family circle®

cooking with
Soy

The Family Circle® Promise of Success

Welcome to the world of Confident Cooking,
created for you in the Australian **Family Circle**®
Test Kitchen, where recipes are double-tested by
our team of home economists to achieve a
high standard of success—and delicious
results every time.

MURDOCH BOOKS®

Sydney • London • Vancouver • New York

All recipes are double-tested by our team of home economists. When we test our recipes, we rate them for ease of preparation. The following cookery ratings are on the recipes in this book, making them easy to use and understand.

A single Cooking with Confidence symbol indicates a recipe that is simple and generally quick to make— perfect for beginners.

Two symbols indicate the need for just a little more care and a little more time.

Three symbols indicate special dishes that need more investment in time, care and patience—but the results are worth it.

TEST KITCHEN PERFECTION

You'll never make a wrong move with a Family Circle step-by-step cookbook. Our team of home economists has tested and refined the recipes so that you can create fabulous food in your own kitchen. Follow our easy instructions and step-by-step photographs and you'll feel like there is a master chef in the kitchen guiding you every step of the way.

IMPORTANT

Those who might be at risk from the effects of salmonella food poisoning (the elderly, pregnant women, young children and those suffering from immune deficiency diseases) should consult their GP with any concerns about eating raw eggs.

The Publisher thanks the following for their assistance: MUD Australia, Ikea, Accoutrement, Sirocco Homewares, Chief Australia, Breville Holdings Pty Ltd, Kambrook, Sheldon & Hammond, Bertolli Olive Oil, Southcorp Appliances.

Front cover: Vietnamese rice paper rolls with dipping sauce (page 28).
Inside front cover: Roast dinner (page 75).
Back cover: Shiitake mushroom and fresh soy bean risotto (page 46).

CONTENTS

Top: Beer-battered tempeh with wedges and avocado aïoli (page 48). **Bottom:** Salmon with miso and soy noodles (page 79), Soy bavarois with mixed berries (page 96).

The story of soy...

There is an ever-increasing tide of information about the many health and nutritional benefits of soy foods, matched by a steady stream of soy-based products appearing on the supermarket shelves. The more we find out about the humble bean, the better the news seems to get.

This book aims to help you incorporate more soy into your diet with a selection of delicious and nutritious recipes from breakfast to dessert. Both vegetarians and meat eaters will find a wealth of ideas to suit their eating habits. This book does not eliminate any particular foods such as eggs or dairy products, but rather uses soy foods in conjunction with more traditional ingredients to help you enjoy the benefits of this versatile bean and its many products without radically changing your diet.

The adaptable bean

The soy bean has many offshoots: it is boiled, puréed, diluted, sweetened and strained to make soy milk; liquefied with water, coagulated, and set to make tofu; fermented to make tempeh; processed into dried bean curd wrappers; sprouted to make soy bean sprouts; salted and fermented to make miso and a variety of sweet and savoury bean pastes; roasted and ground to make a high protein flour; and the oil is extracted for cooking. And that's not all—there is soy-based cheese, cream cheese, yoghurt, ice cream and chocolate which are creeping onto mainstream supermarket shelving systems. If not, try the natural or health food sections.

Health benefits

• Soy beans contain more protein than any other legume, making most soy products an excellent source of non-animal protein.
• With an indirect impact on calcium levels, soy beans enhance calcium retention—animal protein has been shown to increase calcium excretion. Calcium retention is important for maintaining healthy bones.
• Soy beans are also a good source of soluble fibre (which reduces the risk of digestive disorders), omega-3 fatty acids (essential to the functioning of the central nervous system), iron, B vitamins, vitamin E, potassium, zinc and other essential minerals.
• Generally dairy free, soy foods can be enjoyed by people who suffer from lactose intolerance. However, always check the packaging labels as some soy products (like soy cheese) can contain dairy proteins.
• Soy foods can be useful in easing the symptoms of menopause, as they contain phytoestrogens which are believed to help alleviate the effects of low oestrogen production in the body.
• Soy products can also be useful in the dietary treatment of diabetes as they have a low glycemic index and are cholesterol free.

Genetic modification

The debate on genetically modified foods (soy beans among them) has been heated. There is concern about the effects on human health and the environment—on the other hand, it may make production and transportation more cost efficient, bringing cheaper foods to the consumer.

But what is genetic modification? In a nutshell, it introduces, deletes or enhances particular characteristics depending on whether they are 'desirable' or 'undesirable'. New laws regarding the labelling of foods that contain genetically modified ingredients should make it easier for consumers to make the choice between genetically modified or non-modified foods. Many soy foods use non-genetically modified beans; however, some products don't—so check the label carefully before use.

Where the bean began

So where did this wonder bean come from? The soy bean plant is native to China and has been used extensively in Chinese cuisine for over 4,000 years. This small bushy plant bears clusters of hairy seed pods directly attached to the stem. Each pod contains two to three seeds and can be either green, yellow or black.

The soy bean arrived in Europe in 1692, when a German botanist returned from Japan. In 1854, an American expedition to Japan brought back two varieties. But, it wasn't until the 20th century, when scientific research revealed its great nutritional qualities, that the bean was embraced.

There are over a thousand known varieties of soy beans but very few are marketed commercially. Two main varieties are grown in western countries—one for commercial use and the other for eating fresh or dried.

Tips on soy products

• Soy milks can vary greatly, brand to brand—some are sweeter and creamier than others. They can be purchased malt-free, calcium-enriched, fresh or in long-life tetra packs, as well as in different flavours.
• Each form of tofu is different in texture and responds differently to particular cooking methods—ensure you buy the most suitable product for your purpose. Textures and flavours also vary between brands.
• For the purposes of this book, soy spread (or soy margarine) and soy butter are NOT interchangeable. Soy butter is suitable for rubbing into flour for pastries or crumbles, but not for melting—soy margarine is best for this.
• Soy cheeses also vary in texture and flavour. They can be very soft and creamy, as well as firm and rubbery. Some are flavoured with herbs and spices.
• Soy flour doesn't contain the gluten which gives structure to yeast-raised breads, so it can't replace all the wheat or rye flour in a recipe. The balance of soy flour to wheat flour has been carefully tested to achieve the best results while maintaining the soy content. In some recipes, gluten flour has been added to improve the texture of certain baked products.

glossary

If you thought the only soy-based product around was tofu, then you will be pleasantly surprised by the amazing range of products and ingredients made from soy beans. They are becoming more popular and, therefore, more accessible. But, not all the entries in this glossary are soy-based—there are other 'unusual' ingredients used in the following recipes. As a general note, they should all be available in supermarkets, health food stores or specialist shops.

BEAN CURD SHEETS: fried bean curd skin which is available seasoned or unseasoned. Available pre-split to use as pouches for inari sushi, or unsplit to be sliced in soups and other dishes. Available in Asian grocery stores.

GLUTEN FLOUR: gluten is a wheat protein that gives structure to yeast-raised breads. It can be added to soy flour (which has no gluten) to improve the texture of baked foods.

BLACK BEANS: a black soy bean, available dried, fermented, salted and canned in brine. Do not confuse with turtle beans (sometimes labelled as black beans) which are used in South American cooking.

GROUND BEAN SAUCE (tim mein jeung): is made from fermented soy beans which are then ground into a smooth paste. It has a sweet and salty flavour with a long shelf life.

CHILLI BEAN PASTE: made from fermented soy beans, this is often labelled as chilli bean sauce despite its thick consistency. It should be used sparingly and has a long shelf life.

LECITHIN MEAL: is a mixture of lecithin, raw wheat germ and wholemeal flour. Lecithin is a nutrient extracted from soy beans that plays a beneficial role in fat and cholesterol metabolism.

LSA MIX: is a combination of linseed, sunflower seeds and almonds. LSA mix is available ground and in seed form—ground LSA mix should be stored in a sealed container in the refrigerator. Available from health food stores.

SOY BEANS (FRESH): the fresh beans or whole, young pods are available frozen from Asian grocery stores. Depending on seasonal conditions, they are sometimes available fresh.

MISO: a protein-rich paste made from fermented soy beans and grains. Yellow and white miso pastes have a mild flavour, while red and brown pastes are saltier and more pungent.

SOY BEAN SPROUTS: soy beans can be sprouted and used in the same way as other bean sprouts. They can grow up to twice the size of mung bean sprouts, with a stronger flavour and coarser texture.

SOY BEANS (CANNED): these soy beans are pre-cooked and packed in brine and should be rinsed well before using. Soy beans provide the best quality protein of all pulses.

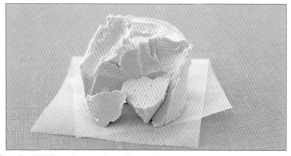

SOY BUTTER: is made of soy bean extract and vegetable oil. It can be used as a spread and for baking purposes, but is not appropriate for melting. It is cholesterol and lactose free.

SOY BEANS (DRIED): small, oval, yellow beans that require soaking before cooking. They require a longer cooking time than most other beans—usually around 2 hours, depending on the size of the bean.

SOY CHEESE/SOY CREAM CHEESE: soy cheeses vary in texture (creamy, soft or firm) and flavour (combined with herbs and spices). Soy cheeses do not contain lactose, therefore do not brown well.

glossary

SOY CHOCOLATE: is a combination of soy extract and cocoa liquor. It is dairy, lactose and cholesterol free—great for those who are lactose intolerant and love their chocolate.

SOY MILK: is available in thin or creamy textures, calcium or vitamin fortified, fat reduced, malt free and in a variety of flavours. Available fresh or in long life cartons. Check the labels as some brands have added sweeteners.

SOY FLOUR: is made from roasted soy beans that have been ground into a fine powder. It is rich in protein and is gluten free. Because of its short shelf life, store soy flour in an airtight container in the refrigerator.

SOY OIL: a natural oil extracted from whole soy beans that can be used as a cooking or salad oil. It is cholesterol free and contains omega-3 fatty acids—essential for nervous system functioning and reducing the risk of heart disease.

SOY GRITS: whole soy beans that have been lightly toasted and cracked into small pieces. They need to be soaked before using. Pre-soaked grits will keep in the refrigerator for 4 days in a sealed container.

SOY PASTA: contains soy flour and added soy proteins in addition to the usual durum wheat flour. Available in supermarkets and health food stores.

SOY MAYONNAISE: is made from soy beans, soy bean oil and seasoned with vinegar, sugar and salt—some contain eggs. It is available in different flavours such as herb or garlic.

SOY SPREAD OR MARGARINE: is made from soy bean oil and is predominantly polyunsaturated. Use as a spread and in cooking. Appropriate when melting is required.

SOY YOGHURT: is made from soy milk and added cultures. Its consistency varies from brand to brand—some are quite thick while others are runny. It is available in many different flavours or plain.

TOFU (FRIED PUFFS): are cubes of tofu which have been aerated and deep-fried. They are suitable for use in stir-fries, curries, laksas and soups. They are available from Asian food stores.

TEMPEH: is made by mixing hulled and slightly split soy beans with a vegetarian fermenting agent. The beans are then bound together to form a firm cake. Is available plain or seasoned.

TOFU (HARD): a harder, compressed and salted version of firm tofu. It holds its shape during cooking. Refrigerate leftover tofu in a sealed container filled with water—it will keep up to 5 days if the water is changed every second day.

TOFU DESSERT: a layer of creamy silken tofu topped with a layer of fruit (several flavours are available) and is usually available in 200 g tubs. Eaten straight from the tub or used as an ingredients in desserts such as bavarois.

TOFU (SILKEN): has a smooth silky texture and, when blended, is similar to cream. It doesn't stir-fry well due to its delicate texture and is often added to soups in cubes, or blended in desserts and smoothies.

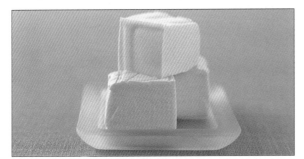

TOFU (FIRM): it holds its shape when cooking and can be sliced, cubed and crumbled—use in stir-fries, pan-fries and baking. Blending is not recommended.

TOFU (SILKEN FIRM): this has the same smooth, custard-like texture as silken tofu only firmer. When blended, the texture is similar to a heavy cream or yoghurt. Can be deep-fried and used in soups.

BREAKFAST

SOY PANCAKES WITH RASPBERRIES AND MAPLE SYRUP

Preparation time: 10 minutes +
  15 minutes standing
Total cooking time: 20 minutes
Serves 4–6

1 cup (125 g) plain flour
1/2 cup (50 g) soy flour
1 tablespoon baking powder
2 tablespoons sugar
1/4 cup (65 g) silken tofu
1 3/4 cups (425 ml) vanilla soy milk
50 g soy spread or margarine, melted
  and cooled
500 g raspberries
1/2 cup (125 ml) maple syrup
icing sugar, for dusting

1 Sift the plain and soy flours, baking powder and 1/2 teaspoon salt together in a large bowl, then stir in the sugar. Place the tofu, soy milk and 1 tablespoon of the melted soy spread in a food processor and combine until the mixture is smooth. Add to the dry ingredients and mix together well. Cover with plastic wrap and leave for 15 minutes.
2 Heat some of the remaining soy spread in a frying pan over medium heat. Making two pancakes at a time, drop 2 tablespoons of the batter in the pan per pancake and cook for 1–2 minutes, or until bubbles form on the surface. Turn and cook the other side for 1 minute, or until golden. Keep warm and repeat with the remaining batter to make 12 pancakes in total.
3 To make the syrup, place the raspberries and maple syrup in a saucepan and stir to coat. Gently cook for 1–2 minutes, or until the berries are warm and well coated in the syrup.
4 Place 2 or 3 pancakes on each plate, top with the maple raspberries and dust with the icing sugar.

NUTRITION PER SERVE (6)
Protein 9 g; Fat 12 g; Carbohydrate 50 g;
Dietary Fibre 6 g; Cholesterol 0 mg;
1372 kJ (328 cal)

COOK'S FILE
Notes: The raspberry is a fruiting plant which grows wild in all the cooler regions of the northern hemisphere, and is related to the blackberry—both raspberries and blackberries can range in colour from white to yellow, orange, pink, red, purple and black.
Variation: Any berries such as blackberries, blueberries or strawberries can be used instead of raspberries, if desired.
Storage: Raspberries should be stored covered, but unwashed, in the refrigerator.

Blend the tofu, soy milk and soy spread in a food processor until smooth.

Cook the pancakes until small bubbles appear on the surface.

BIRCHER MUESLI

Preparation time: 10 minutes +
  overnight soaking
Total cooking time: 8 minutes
Serves 6–8

1 cup (250 ml) fresh orange juice
2 tablespoons maple syrup
1 teaspoon vanilla essence
100 g silken tofu
1½ cups (150 g) rolled oats
½ cup (60 g) slivered almonds
½ cup (80 g) sultanas
1 cup (250 g) vanilla soy yoghurt
200 g mixed fresh fruit

1 Combine the orange juice, maple syrup, vanilla essence and tofu in a food processor until well combined—the mixture will be slightly grainy.
2 Place the oats in a large bowl. Pour the tofu mixture over the oats and stir well. Cover with plastic wrap and soak overnight in the refrigerator.
3 Preheat the oven to warm 170°C (325°F/Gas 3). Spread the almonds evenly on a baking tray and toast for 5–8 minutes, or until golden.
4 Before serving, add the sultanas and toasted almonds to the oat mixture and stir to combine. Serve topped with the vanilla soy yoghurt and mixed fruit.

NUTRITION PER SERVE (8)
Protein 6 g; Fat 6.5 g; Carbohydrate 30 g; Dietary Fibre 2 g; Cholesterol 0 mg; 825 kJ (197 cal)

COOK'S FILE
Note: Originally served with milk, this Swiss–German dish is named after Dr Bircher-Benner who served it to patients at his natural health clinic in Zurich.

Add the tofu and orange juice mixture to the oats and stir well.

Toast the slivered almonds in a warm oven until golden.

BANANA BREAD

Preparation time: 15 minutes +
  overnight resting
Total cooking time: 1 hour
Serves 6

125 g soy butter
3/4 cup (140 g) soft brown sugar
2 eggs
3/4 cup (90 g) self-raising flour
1/4 cup (20 g) soy flour
1/2 teaspoon bicarbonate of soda
1 teaspoon vanilla essence
3 ripe bananas, mashed (660 g)

1/2 cup (60 g) walnuts, chopped
icing sugar, for dusting
fresh fruit, to serve
vanilla soy yoghurt, to serve

1 Preheat the oven to moderate 180°C (350°F/Gas 4). Grease a 10 x 20 cm loaf tin and line the base with baking paper.
2 Beat the soy butter and sugar with electric beaters until smooth and creamy. Add the eggs one at a time, beating well after each addition. Sift the self-raising and soy flours with the bicarbonate of soda and add to the egg and butter mixture with the vanilla and banana. Fold the walnuts into the mixture using a metal spoon.
3 Spoon the bread mixture into the prepared tin and bake for 1 hour, or until a skewer comes out clean when inserted into the centre of the bread. Cool slightly, then transfer to a wire rack. When completely cold, wrap in foil and leave overnight.
4 Cut into thick slices and toast to your liking. Dust with icing sugar and serve with fresh fruit and a dollop of vanilla soy yoghurt.

NUTRITION PER SERVE
Protein 7 g; Fat 30 g; Carbohydrate 46 g;
Dietary Fibre 3 g; Cholesterol 60 mg;
1988 kJ (475 cal)

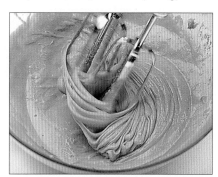

Beat the eggs one at a time into the creamed soy butter and sugar mixture.

Fold the walnuts into the bread mixture until well incorporated.

Spoon the mixture into the greased and lined loaf tin.

BREAKFAST IN A GLASS

STRAWBERRY SOY LASSI
Blend *250 g fresh strawberries, 300 g strawberry soy yoghurt, 2 tablespoons honey, 50 ml water* and *4 ice cubes* in a blender until smooth. Makes 2 x 250 ml glasses.

FRESH DATE AND PEAR SHAKE
Blend *400 ml creamy soy milk, 4 fresh chopped dates* and *2 small ripe chopped pears* in a blender until smooth. Makes 2 x 350 ml glasses.

CAROB PEANUT SMOOTHIE
Blend *400 ml carob or chocolate soy milk drink, 2 very ripe chopped bananas, 150 g silken tofu, 2 tablespoons honey* and *1 tablespoon peanut butter* in a blender until smooth. Makes 3 x 250 ml glasses.

SPICED MELON SHAKE
Lightly crush *1/4 teaspoon cardamom seeds* in a mortar and pestle or with the back of a knife. Place in a blender with *350 ml creamy soy milk* and blend for 30 seconds. Strain the soy milk and rinse any remaining seeds from the blender. Return the strained milk to the blender, add *250 g chopped rockmelon, 1 tablespoon honey, 2 tablespoons ground almonds* and *4 ice cubes* and blend until smooth. Makes 2 x 300 ml glasses.

TROPICAL MORNING SMOOTHIE
Blend *2 chopped mangoes (400 g), 350 ml creamy soy milk, 150 ml pineapple juice, 1/4 cup (15 g) chopped fresh mint* and *6 ice cubes* in a blender until smooth. Garnish with a sprig of fresh mint. Makes 3 x 300 ml glasses.

MAPLE BANANA BREAKFAST
Blend *350 ml fresh or creamy soy milk, 150 g vanilla soy yoghurt, 2 very ripe chopped bananas, 1 large ripe chopped yellow peach, 2 teaspoons lecithin meal* and *2 tablespoons maple syrup* in a blender until smooth. Makes 2 x 375 ml glasses.

Clockwise from top left: Strawberry soy lassi, Fresh date and pear shake, Carob peanut smoothie, Spiced melon shake, Tropical morning smoothie and Maple banana breakfast.

Simmer, stirring occasionally, until the barley is soft.

Sauté the apple pieces in a frying pan for 2 minutes.

Cook the apple and sugar mixture until the sugar dissolves and caramelises.

BARLEY WITH CARAMELISED APPLE

Preparation time: 15 minutes
Total cooking time: 45 minutes
Serves 4

1.4 litres soy milk
2 cups (440 g) pearl barley
50 g soy spread or margarine
4 apples, peeled and cut into
   2 cm cubes
1/2 cup (80 g) sultanas
1 teaspoon ground cinnamon
1/4 teaspoon ground nutmeg
pinch ground cloves
1 teaspoon vanilla essence
1/2 cup (95 g) soft brown sugar

1/2 cup (45 g) desiccated coconut
2 tablespoons roasted and chopped
   macadamia nuts

1 Place the soy milk, pearl barley and a pinch of salt in a saucepan. Simmer over medium heat, stirring occasionally, for 30 minutes, or until the barley is soft.
2 Melt the soy spread in a frying pan over medium heat. Add the apple and sauté for 2 minutes. Add the sultanas, cinnamon, nutmeg, ground cloves and vanilla essence and sauté for a further 2 minutes. Add the sugar and cook for 10 minutes, or until the sugar has dissolved and the apple has caramelised.
3 Add the apple mixture to the barley and cook over medium heat

for 1 minute, or until warmed through. Serve topped with the coconut and macadamia nuts.

NUTRITION PER SERVE
Protein 22 g; Fat 40 g; Carbohydrate 143 g; Dietary Fibre 17 g; Cholesterol 0 mg; 3884 kJ (928 cal)

COOK'S FILE
Note: Barley is the oldest cultivated cereal in the Near East and Europe and, during ancient times, was the primary staple grain. Porridge made with barley is more delicate than oatmeal porridge and is usually made with milk (or soy milk in this case) rather than water.

CORN CAKES WITH TOMATO SALSA

Preparation time: 15 minutes
Total cooking time: 15 minutes
Serves 4

Tomato salsa
2 tablespoons diced red onion
2 firm tomatoes, seeded and diced
1/2 Lebanese cucumber, seeded and diced
2 tablespoons fresh flat-leaf parsley, chopped
1 tablespoon soy bean oil
1 tablespoon white vinegar

4 fresh corn cobs or 425 g can corn kernels, drained

2 spring onions, finely chopped
2 eggs, lightly beaten
3/4 cup (75 g) soy flour
1/3 cup (40 g) plain flour
3/4 cup (185 ml) soy milk
3 tablespoons soy bean oil

1 To make the tomato salsa, place the red onion, tomato, cucumber and parsley in a bowl. Season with salt and freshly ground black pepper, then add the soy oil and vinegar and toss together well to coat.
2 If using fresh corn, remove the kernels by cutting down the length of the cob with a sharp knife. Place the kernels in a small bowl with the spring onion and combine.
3 Whisk together the egg, soy and plain flours and soy milk in a bowl. Fold in the corn and spring onion mixture and season to taste with salt and freshly ground black pepper.
4 Heat the soy oil in a frying pan over medium heat. Working in batches, drop 2 tablespoons of batter per corn cake into the pan and allow enough space for spreading. Cook over medium heat for 2 minutes, or until golden. Turn over and cook for a further 1–2 minutes, or until golden. Repeat with the remaining batter to make 12 corn cakes.
5 To serve, stack three corn cakes on individual plates and top with some tomato salsa.

NUTRITION PER SERVE
Protein 14 g; Fat 28 g; Carbohydrate 30 g; Dietary Fibre 8 g; Cholesterol 90 mg; 1988 kJ (403 cal)

Cut down the length of the cob with a sharp knife to remove the kernels.

Fold the corn and spring onion mixture through the batter.

Cook the corn cakes until golden brown on both sides.

SCRAMBLED TOFU WITH MUSHROOMS

Preparation time: 10 minutes
Total cooking time: 15 minutes
Serves 4

40 g soy spread or margarine
200 g button mushrooms, sliced
1 clove garlic, crushed
2 spring onions, chopped
400 g firm tofu, drained and
    crumbled
1 teaspoon tamari
1 tablespoon finely chopped fresh
    parsley
8 thick slices soy and linseed bread

1 Melt 1 tablespoon of the soy spread in a large frying pan. Add the mushrooms and cook over high heat for 5 minutes, or until the mushrooms start to lose their moisture. Add the garlic and cook for a further 5 minutes, or until the liquid has evaporated. Remove from the pan.
2 Melt the remaining soy spread in the pan. Add the spring onion and cook for 30 seconds, or until just wilted. Add the tofu, tamari and mushrooms and cook, stirring gently, for 2 minutes, or until the tofu is heated through. Stir in the parsley and season with black pepper.
3 Lightly toast the bread, spread with a little soy butter, if desired, and serve with the scrambled tofu.

NUTRITION PER SERVE
Protein 15 g; Fat 16 g; Carbohydrate 25 g; Dietary Fibre 5.5 g; Cholesterol 0 mg; 1280 kJ (306 cal)

Drain the tofu and crumble into a bowl, using your fingers.

Cook the mushrooms and garlic until the moisture has evaporated.

Add the spring onion to the pan and cook until it is soft and wilted.

SAVOURY FRENCH TOAST WITH FRIED TOMATOES

Preparation time: 10 minutes
Total cooking time: 30 minutes
Serves 4

4 vine-ripened tomatoes
1 teaspoon sugar
1 tablespoon soy bean oil
1½ cups (200 g) grated soy cheese
¼ cup (5 g) lightly packed fresh
   basil
8 slices soy and linseed bread
   (see Note)
2 eggs
¼ cup (60 ml) soy milk

25 g soy spread or margarine
fresh basil sprigs, to garnish

1 Preheat the oven to warm 160°C (315°F/Gas 2–3). Cut the tomatoes in half, sprinkle with sugar and season. Heat 1 teaspoon of the oil in a stainless steel frying pan. Add the tomatoes cut-side-down and fry over high heat for 1–2 minutes, or until a crust has formed. Place on a baking tray and bake for 10 minutes. Wipe the pan clean.
2 Divide the cheese and basil evenly among 4 slices of bread, then top with the remaining bread slices. Pat down well to form a tight sandwich (remove the crusts, if desired).
3 Beat the eggs and milk together in

a bowl, then season well. Dip the sandwiches in the egg mixture until saturated but not soggy.
4 Heat the soy spread and remaining oil in the pan. Cook the sandwiches over medium heat for 2 minutes each side, or until crisp and golden.
5 Cut the sandwiches in half and arrange one triangle leaning against the other. Serve with the tomatoes.

NUTRITION PER SERVE
Protein 23 g; Fat 35 g; Carbohydrate 27 g;
Dietary Fibre 5.5 g; Cholesterol 140 mg;
2056 kJ (490 cal)

COOK'S FILE
Note: Day-old bread is preferable when making French toast, as it will not absorb as much liquid as fresh bread.

Fry the tomato halves until a crust has formed on the base.

Dip the sandwiches in the egg mixture until well coated, but not soggy.

Fry the sandwiches on both sides until crisp and golden.

LUNCH

LENTIL SOUP WITH SPICED YOGHURT

Preparation time: 10 minutes
Total cooking time: 25 minutes
Serves 4–6

1 tablespoon soy bean oil
1 large onion, finely chopped
2 cloves garlic, crushed
1 teaspoon ground cumin
1/2 teaspoon garam masala
1/2 teaspoon sambal oelek
1/4 cup (60 g) tomato paste
1 cup (250 g) red lentils
1 teaspoon sugar
415 g can crushed tomatoes
3 cups (375 ml) vegetable stock
1/2 cup (125 g) plain soy yoghurt
2 tablespoons fresh coriander
    leaves
fresh coriander sprigs, to garnish

Spiced yoghurt
1 cup (250 g) plain soy yoghurt
2 tablespoons chopped fresh
    coriander leaves
1/2 teaspoon ground coriander
1/2 teaspoon ground cumin
1/2 teaspoon mild paprika

1 Heat the oil in a saucepan. Add the onion and cook over medium heat for 1 minute. Stir in the garlic, cumin, garam masala and sambal oelek and cook for 30 seconds more, or until fragrant. Add the tomato paste, lentils, sugar, crushed tomatoes, stock and 1 cup (250 ml) water to the saucepan and simmer for 20 minutes, or until the lentils are tender.
2 Remove half the soup and leave to cool slightly—keep the remaining warm in the pan over low heat (be careful not to boil). Place the cooled portion in a food processor or blender, add the yoghurt and coriander leaves and blend together until smooth. Add the blended mixture to the remaining soup and stir well to combine. Keep warm over low heat—do not reboil.
3 To make the spiced yoghurt, combine the yoghurt, fresh and ground coriander, cumin and paprika in a bowl, just before serving.
4 Serve the soup in individual soup bowls with a dollop of spiced yoghurt and garnish with a sprig of coriander.

NUTRITION PER SERVE (6)
Protein 12 g; Fat 3 g; Carbohydrate 20 g; Dietary Fibre 6 g; Cholesterol 0 mg; 653 kJ (156 cal)

COOK'S FILE
Note: This soup can sometimes have a slightly curdled appearance due to the yoghurt, but it in no way detracts from the flavour of the dish.

Simmer the soup over medium heat until the lentils are tender.

Spoon half the soup into a food processor and blend until smooth.

CARROT AND LEEK TART

Preparation time: 35 minutes +
40 minutes chilling
Total cooking time:
1 hour 35 minutes
Serves 6–8

200 g russet (Idaho) potatoes,
quartered
1 tablespoon soy milk
1 cup (150 g) wholemeal flour
1/2 cup (50 g) soy flour
150 g soy spread or margarine
2 carrots (450 g), cut into small pieces
2 leeks (450 g), trimmed and thinly
sliced
1 cup (250 ml) vegetable stock
1/2 teaspoon sugar
1 tablespoon tomato paste
3 eggs
200 g plain soy yoghurt
1 small carrot, extra
1 small leek, extra
1 tablespoon soy spread or
margarine, extra

1 Boil the potato in a saucepan of salted water for 8–10 minutes, or until tender. Drain well, return to the pan, add the soy milk and season. Mash until smooth, then cool.
2 Place the flours in a bowl and rub in 100 g of the soy spread until it resembles fine breadcrumbs. Add the potato and bring together to form a ball. Cool, then wrap in plastic wrap. Refrigerate for at least 30 minutes.
3 Preheat the oven to moderately hot 200°C (400°F/Gas 6). Roll out the dough and line a 23 cm tart tin with a removable base with the pastry and trim. Chill for 10 minutes. Line the pastry with baking paper and fill

with baking beads or uncooked rice. Bake for 15 minutes. Remove the baking paper and beads and bake for 5 minutes, or until slightly golden. Reduce the oven to moderate 180°C (350°F/Gas 4).
4 Melt the remaining soy spread in a saucepan. Add the carrot, leek and 2 tablespoons water and sauté gently for 10 minutes, or until the liquid has evaporated. Add the stock and sugar and cook for 20 minutes, or until tender and all the liquid has been absorbed. Cool slightly, then add the paste, eggs and yoghurt. Place in a

food processor and blend until smooth. Season. Pour into the pastry case and bake for 20–25 minutes, or until set and lightly golden on top.
5 Peel the extra carrot into thin ribbons with a vegetable peeler. Slice the extra leek lengthways into thin ribbons. Melt the extra soy spread in a frying pan. Add the carrot and leek and sauté for 8 minutes, or until soft. Pile in the centre of the tart and serve.

NUTRITION PER SERVE (8)
Protein 6 g; Fat 24 g; Carbohydrate 17 g;
Dietary Fibre 4.5 g; Cholesterol 68 mg;
1266 kJ (302 cal)

Combine the flours and soy spread with your fingers until it resembles breadcrumbs.

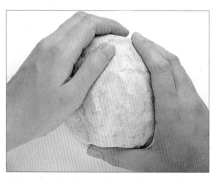

Bring the dough together to form a ball, then wrap and refrigerate.

Cook the carrot, leek, stock and sugar until all the liquid has been absorbed.

SOY AND MUSHROOM BURGERS

Preparation time: 25 minutes
Total cooking time: 15 minutes
Serves 4

2 tablespoons soy bean oil
1 onion, finely chopped
200 g field or cap mushrooms, finely chopped
1 clove garlic, crushed
420 g can soy beans, rinsed and drained
1½ cups (120 g) fresh wholemeal breadcrumbs
2 teaspoons fresh thyme, chopped

1 egg, lightly beaten
4 Turkish bread rolls
1 avocado, mashed
60 g mixed lettuce leaves
purchased tomato chutney, to serve

1 Heat 2 teaspoons of the oil in a frying pan. Add the onion and cook, stirring occasionally, over medium heat for 3 minutes, or until soft. Add the mushrooms and garlic and cook, stirring, for 2 minutes, or until just soft. Cool slightly.
2 Place the soy beans in a large bowl and roughly mash with a potato masher. Add the mushroom mixture, breadcrumbs, thyme and beaten egg. Season well with salt and freshly ground black pepper and stir until combined. With wet hands, shape the mixture into 4 patties about 10 cm in diameter.
3 Heat the remaining oil in a frying pan. Cook the patties, in batches, for 2–3 minutes each side, or until golden brown—they will be quite fragile, so handle carefully during cooking.
4 To assemble, split the rolls and toast on both sides. Spread the base with the mashed avocado, top with the lettuce, a burger patty and a dollop of chutney.

NUTRITION PER SERVE
Protein 50 g; Fat 42 g; Carbohydrate 73 g; Dietary Fibre 28 g; Cholesterol 45 mg; 3683 kJ (880 cal)

Roughly mash the canned soy beans with a potato masher.

Form the soy and mushroom mixture into 10 cm round patties.

Fry the patties in batches until both sides are golden brown.

23

TOFU AND VEGETABLE KOFTAS WITH YOGHURT DIPPING SAUCE

Preparation time: 25 minutes
Total cooking time: 20 minutes
Serves 4

Yoghurt dipping sauce
200 g plain soy yoghurt
1 clove garlic, crushed
2 tablespoons fresh mint, finely chopped

250 g firm tofu
4 tablespoons olive oil
1½ cups (185 g) grated pumpkin (see Note)
¾ cup (100 g) grated zucchini (see Note)
1 onion, chopped
4 cloves garlic, crushed
4 small spring onions, finely chopped
¼ cup (7 g) chopped fresh coriander leaves
1 tablespoon Madras curry powder
1 cup (150 g) wholemeal flour
½ cup (50 g) grated Parmesan
oil, for deep-frying

1 To make the dipping sauce, place the yoghurt, garlic and mint in a small bowl, season and mix together well. Add a little water, if needed.
2 Blend the tofu in a food processor or blender until finely processed.
3 Heat the oil in a frying pan. Add the pumpkin, zucchini, onion and garlic and cook over medium heat, stirring occasionally, for 10 minutes, or until the vegetables are tender. Leave to cool.
4 Add the spring onion, coriander, curry powder, ½ cup (75 g) of the wholemeal flour, Parmesan, tofu and 1 tablespoon salt and mix well. Roll a tablespoon of the mixture between your hands to form a ball, then repeat with the remaining mixture. Coat the balls in the remaining flour.
5 Fill a deep heavy-based saucepan one third full of oil and heat to 180°C (350°F), or until a cube of bread browns in 15 seconds. Cook the tofu and vegetable koftas in small batches for 2–3 minutes, or until golden brown. Drain on paper towels. Serve with the dipping sauce.

NUTRITION PER SERVE
Protein 20 g; Fat 20 g; Carbohydrate 30 g; Dietary Fibre 7.5 g; Cholesterol 20 mg; 1553 kJ (370 cal)

COOK'S FILE
Note: When buying the vegetables, buy a piece of pumpkin that weighs about 400 g and about 200 g zucchini.

Cook the pumpkin, zucchini, onion and garlic until tender.

Roll tablespoons of the tofu and vegetable mixture into balls.

Deep-fry the koftas in small batches until golden brown all over.

TABBOULEH WITH SOY GRITS

Preparation time: 20 minutes +
  soaking
Total cooking time: Nil
Serves 6–8

150 g fresh flat-leaf parsley
1 cup (180 g) soy grits
2 tablespoons chopped fresh mint
1 small red onion, cut into thin
  wedges

3 ripe tomatoes, chopped
400 g can chickpeas, rinsed and
  drained
3 tablespoons lemon juice
2 tablespoons extra virgin olive oil
Lebanese or pitta bread, to serve

1   Remove all the parsley leaves from
the stalks, roughly chop and place in
a large serving bowl.
2   Place the soy grits in a heatproof
bowl and pour in 2/3 cup (170 ml)
boiling water. Leave to soak for
3 minutes, or until all the water has
been absorbed.

3   Add the soy grits to the parsley,
along with the mint, onion, tomato
and chickpeas. Drizzle with the
lemon juice and olive oil. Season well
with salt and freshly ground black
pepper and toss together.
4   Serve with Lebanese or pitta bread
and Soy bean hummus (see page 33)
as a vegetarian meal, or as an
accompaniment to barbecued meat,
chicken or fish.

NUTRITION PER SERVE (8)
Protein 12 g; Fat 11 g; Carbohydrate 13 g;
Dietary Fibre 6.5 g; Cholesterol 0 mg;
820 kJ (196 cal)

Cut the red onion into thin wedges with a sharp knife.

Allow the grits and water to soak until the liquid has been absorbed.

Toss together the grits, parsley, mint, onion, tomato, chickpeas and dressing.

PARMESAN-CRUSTED TEMPEH

Preparation time: 25 minutes +
   40 minutes refrigeration
Total cooking time: 45 minutes
Serves 4

300 g tempeh
4 tablespoons plain flour
4 tablespoons finely chopped fresh
   flat-leaf parsley
1 cup (80 g) fresh breadcrumbs
1/2 cup (50 g) freshly grated Parmesan
2 eggs, beaten
2–3 tablespoons soy bean oil

Tomato sauce
1 tablespoon soy bean oil
2 tablespoons finely chopped onion
800 g ripe tomatoes, peeled, seeded
   and chopped
1 tablespoon balsamic vinegar
1 teaspoon sugar
2 teaspoons fresh oregano, chopped

1 Cut the tempeh into 8 fingers. Season the flour with salt and freshly ground black pepper. Combine the parsley, breadcrumbs and Parmesan and season. Coat the tempeh in the flour, dip in the egg, then coat in the breadcrumbs. Place on a foil-lined tray and refrigerate for 20 minutes. Dip the crumbed fingers in the egg again, coat with a second layer of breadcrumbs, then refrigerate for a further 20 minutes.
2 To make the sauce, heat the oil in a saucepan. Add the onion and cook over medium heat for 5–8 minutes, or until just golden. Add the tomato and simmer, stirring frequently, for 20 minutes, or until thickened. Add the vinegar, sugar and oregano. Cook for a further 2 minutes. Keep warm.
3 Preheat the oven to very slow 120°C (250°F/Gas 1/2). Heat the oil in a frying pan. Fry the tempeh in batches for 3 minutes on each side, or until browned. Keep warm in the oven between batches. Serve with a little sauce on the side and a salad, if desired.

NUTRITION PER SERVE
Protein 20 g; Fat 15 g; Carbohydrate 27 g;
Dietary Fibre 4.5 g; Cholesterol 96 mg;
1376 kJ (329 cal)

Use a sharp knife to cut the tempeh into 8 even-sized fingers.

Coat the tempeh in the flour, egg and then the Parmesan and breadcrumb mixture.

Simmer the sauce, stirring frequently, until it has thickened.

Fry the Parmesan-crusted tempeh until both sides are golden brown.

Roughly crush the cumin seeds in a mortar and pestle.

Whisk the mixture together to form a smooth batter.

Deep-fry the pakoras in small batches until they are pale gold.

VEGETABLE PAKORAS WITH SPICED YOGHURT

Preparation time: 30 minutes +
15 minutes standing
Total cooking time: 20 minutes
Serves 4

Spiced yoghurt
1 teaspoon cumin seeds
200 g plain soy yoghurt
1 clove garlic, crushed
1/2 cup (15 g) fresh coriander leaves, chopped

1/3 cup (35 g) besan (chickpea flour)
1/3 cup (40 g) self-raising flour
1/3 cup (45 g) soy flour
1/2 teaspoon ground turmeric
1 teaspoon cayenne pepper
1/2 teaspoon ground coriander
1 small fresh green chilli, seeded and finely chopped
oil, for deep-frying
200 g cauliflower, cut into small florets

140 g orange sweet potato, cut into 5 mm slices
180 g eggplant, cut into 5 mm slices
180 g fresh asparagus, cut into 6 cm lengths

1 To make the spiced yoghurt, heat a small frying pan over medium heat. Add the cumin seeds and deep-fry for 1–2 minutes, or until aromatic—shake the pan frequently to prevent the seeds from burning. Place in a mortar and pestle or spice grinder and roughly grind. Whisk into the soy yoghurt with the garlic. Season with salt and freshly ground black pepper, then stir in the coriander.
2 Place the besan, self-raising and soy flours, ground turmeric, cayenne pepper, ground coriander, chilli and 1 teaspoon salt in a bowl. Gradually whisk in 1 cup (250 ml) cold water to form a batter. Leave for 15 minutes. Preheat the oven to very slow 120°C (250°F/Gas 1/2).
3 Fill a small saucepan one third full with oil and heat to 170°C (325°F),

or until a cube of bread browns in 20 seconds. Dip the vegetables in the batter and deep-fry in small batches, for 1–2 minutes, or until pale gold. Remove with a slotted spoon and drain on paper towels. Keep warm in the oven until all the vegetables are deep-fried.
5 Serve the hot vegetable pakoras with the spiced yoghurt and a green salad, if desired.

NUTRITION PER SERVE
Protein 11 g; Fat 15 g; Carbohydrate 17 g; Dietary Fibre 6 g; Cholesterol 0 mg; 1025 kJ (245 cal)

VIETNAMESE RICE PAPER ROLLS WITH DIPPING SAUCE

Preparation time: 40 minutes +
  5 minutes soaking
Total cooking time: 2 minutes
Serves 4

50 g dried rice vermicelli
200 g frozen soy beans
16 square (15 cm) rice paper
  wrappers
1 zucchini, julienned
1 Lebanese cucumber, julienned
1 carrot, grated
1 cup (20 g) fresh mint, julienned
100 g tofu, cut into 1 cm wide batons

Dipping sauce
4 tablespoons fish sauce
2 tablespoons chopped fresh
  coriander leaves
2 small fresh red chillies, finely
  chopped
2 teaspoons soft brown sugar
2 teaspoons lime juice

1 Soak the vermicelli in hot water for 5 minutes, or until soft. Drain and cut into 5 cm lengths with a pair of scissors. Bring a saucepan of water to the boil, add the soy beans and cook for 2 minutes. Drain well.
2 Working with no more than two rice paper wrappers at a time, dip each wrapper in a bowl of warm water for 10 seconds to soften. Drain, then lay out on a flat work surface.
3 Place a small amount of rice vermicelli on the bottom third of a wrapper, leaving a 2 cm border either side. Top with a little zucchini, cucumber, carrot, soy beans, mint and 2 batons of tofu. Keeping the filling compact and neat, fold in both sides and roll up tightly. Seal with a little water, if necessary. Cover with a damp cloth and repeat with the remaining rice paper wrappers and filling ingredients.
4 To make the dipping sauce, place the fish sauce, coriander leaves, chilli, brown sugar, lime juice and 2 tablespoons water in a small bowl and stir together well. Serve with the rice paper rolls.

NUTRITION PER SERVE
Protein 8 g; Fat 4 g; Carbohydrate 7.5 g;
Dietary Fibre 4 g; Cholesterol 0 mg;
420 kJ (100 cal)

Cut the zucchini and cucumber into julienne strips.

Soak the rice paper wrappers, one at a time, in warm water.

Fold in both sides and roll up the wrapper to enclose the filling.

CHINESE HOT AND SOUR SOUP

Preparation time: 15 minutes +
   30 minutes soaking
Total cooking time: 15 minutes
Serves 4

8 dried shiitake mushrooms
2 teaspoons cornflour
2 teaspoons sesame oil
1 litre vegetable stock
125 g bamboo shoots, julienned
125 g silken firm tofu, cut into
   7.5 cm long thin strips

2 teaspoons light soy sauce
3 tablespoons white wine vinegar
1/2 teaspoon white pepper
spring onions, thinly sliced, to garnish

1 Soak the mushrooms in a bowl with 1/2 cup (125 ml) hot water for 30 minutes. Drain and reserve the liquid in a small bowl. Discard the stems and cut the caps into quarters.
2 Whisk the cornflour, sesame oil and 2 tablespoons of the stock together in a small bowl.
3 Place the remaining stock and reserved mushroom liquid in a large saucepan and bring to the boil. Add the mushrooms and bamboo shoots.

Season with salt, reduce the heat and simmer for 5 minutes.
4 Add the tofu, soy sauce, vinegar and white pepper. Return the soup to a simmer. Stir in the cornflour mixture and cook until the soup thickens slightly. Pour into individual serving bowls and garnish with the spring onion.

NUTRITION PER SERVE
Protein 3.5 g; Fat 4 g; Carbohydrate 6 g;
Dietary Fibre 1 g; Cholesterol 0 mg;
320 kJ (75 cal)

COOK'S FILE
Hint: For a hotter tasting soup, add extra white pepper before serving.

Cut the silken firm tofu into even-sized long thin strips.

Discard the stems, then cut the soaked mushrooms into quarters.

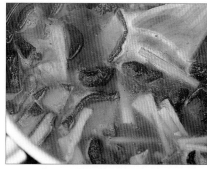

Stir in the cornflour mixture and cook until the soup thickens slightly.

SOY LENTIL BURGERS WITH PEANUT SAUCE

Preparation time: 20 minutes +
 1 hour refrigeration
Total cooking time: 40 minutes
Serves 6

3 tablespoons soy bean oil
1 large brown onion, finely chopped
1 clove garlic, crushed
1 large carrot, finely grated
2 teaspoons mild curry powder
1 cup (250 g) red lentils, washed
2 cups (500 ml) vegetable stock
250 g firm tofu, drained
1/2 cup (15 g) fresh coriander leaves
2 cups (160 g) fresh wholemeal
 breadcrumbs
6 hamburger buns
lettuce leaves, to serve

Peanut sauce
3 tablespoons smooth peanut butter
2 cloves garlic, crushed
1 tablespoon sesame oil
1 tablespoon soy sauce
1 tablespoon sweet chilli sauce
1/2 cup (125 ml) coconut milk

1 Heat 1 tablespoon of the oil in a frying pan. Add the onion and cook over medium heat for 2–3 minutes, or until lightly golden. Add the garlic, carrot and curry powder and cook for a further 1 minute. Stir in the lentils and stock and cook over low heat, stirring occasionally, for 20 minutes, or until the lentils are cooked. Drain well, then allow to cool slightly.
2 Place half the lentil mixture in a food processor. Add the tofu and coriander leaves and process to combine. Transfer to a bowl, add the breadcrumbs and the remaining lentils and mix together to form a thick mixture. Form into 6 large patties, then cover and refrigerate for 1 hour.
3 Heat the remaining oil in a frying pan. Cook the patties in batches, for 3–4 minutes, or until crisp and golden. Turn over and fry the other side for another 3–4 minutes, or until crisp and cooked through.
4 To make the peanut sauce, place the peanut butter, garlic, sesame oil, soy and sweet chilli sauces and coconut milk in a bowl. Stir until it forms a smooth paste—add a little water if it is too thick.
5 Serve the patties on toasted hamburger buns with lettuce leaves and the peanut sauce.

NUTRITION PER SERVE
Protein 28 g; Fat 30 g; Carbohydrate 76 g; Dietary Fibre 12 g ; Cholesterol 0 mg; 2884 kJ (690 cal)

Combine the breadcrumbs and lentil mixture to form a thick consistency.

Fry in batches until the patties are crispy and golden on both sides.

Stir the peanut sauce ingredients together until smooth.

PEAR AND WALNUT SALAD WITH LIME VINAIGRETTE

Preparation time: 25 minutes
Total cooking time: 20 minutes
Serves 4

1 small baguette, cut into 16 thin
    slices
soy bean oil, for brushing
1 clove garlic, cut in half
1 cup (100 g) walnuts
200 g soy cheese
400 g mesclun leaves
2 pears, cut into 2 cm cubes, mixed
    with 2 tablespoons lime juice

Lime vinaigrette
3 tablespoons soy bean oil
1/4 cup (60 ml) lime juice
2 tablespoons raspberry vinegar

1 Preheat the oven to moderate
180°C (350°F/Gas 4). Brush the
baguette slices with a little oil, rub
with the cut side of the garlic, then
place on a baking tray. Bake for
10 minutes, or until crisp and golden.
Place the walnuts on a baking tray
and roast for 5–8 minutes, or until
slightly browned—shake the tray to
ensure even colouring. Allow to cool
for 5 minutes.
2 To make the lime vinaigrette,
whisk together the oil, lime juice,
raspberry vinegar, 1 teaspoon salt and
1/2 teaspoon freshly ground black
pepper in a small bowl. Set aside
until ready to use.
3 Spread some of the soy cheese on
each crouton, then cook under a hot
grill for 2–3 minutes, or until hot.
4 Place the mesclun, pears and
walnuts in a bowl, add the vinaigrette
and toss through. Divide the salad
among four serving bowls and serve
with the soy cheese croutons.

NUTRITION PER SERVE
Protein 24 g; Fat 60 g; Carbohydrate 40 g;
Dietary Fibre 7 g; Cholesterol 0 mg;
3310 kJ (790 cal)

Rub each slice of baguette with a cut piece of garlic.

Whisk together the soy bean oil, lime juice, raspberry vinegar, salt and pepper.

Place the soy cheese-topped croutons on a baking tray and grill until hot.

SNACKS

SESAME-CRUSTED TOFU SNACKS

Cut *300 g firm tofu* into 2 cm cubes. Place *1½ tablespoons white sesame seeds, 1½ tablespoons black sesame seeds* and *2 tablespoons cornflour* on a plate. *Season.* Gently toss the tofu in the sesame seed mixture to coat. Heat *2 tablespoons soy bean oil* in a large, heavy-based frying pan. Fry the tofu in batches over medium heat, turning frequently, for 3–4 minutes, or until toasted on all sides—add a little more oil if necessary. Drain on paper towels. To make the dipping sauce, combine *2 tablespoons light soy sauce, 2 tablespoons mirin* and *1 tablespoon finely chopped fresh ginger*. Serve with the tofu cubes.

AVOCADO AND BLACK BEAN SALSA

Rinse and drain *100 g canned black soy beans*, then place in a bowl with *1 chopped, seeded and diced red capsicum, 1 diced avocado, ½ small diced red onion, 1 cup (50 g) coriander leaves, finely chopped, 1 finely chopped small fresh red chilli* and *2 tablespoons lime juice*, and *season*. Gently toss to combine. Leave for 10 minutes so the flavours infuse. Serve with soy chips.

SOY BEAN HUMMUS

Soak *125 g dried soy beans* in plenty of water overnight. Drain and cook in a large saucepan of boiling water for 1½–2 hours, or until tender. Drain. Heat *1 tablespoon soy bean oil* in a frying pan and cook *1 small finely chopped onion* over medium heat for 5–8 minutes, or until soft. Add *1½ teaspoons ground cumin* and *a pinch of cayenne pepper* and cook over high heat for 1 minute, or until aromatic. Stir in the soy beans to coat. Place the mixture in a food processor with *2 tablespoons lemon juice, ½ cup (125 ml) olive oil* and *2 crushed cloves garlic*, season with *salt* and process until smooth—add a little *water* for a thinner consistency. Makes about 2 cups (500 ml). Can be made up to 5 days ahead and stored in an airtight container in the refrigerator.

CRUNCHY SPICED SOY BEANS

Soak *100 g dried soy beans* in plenty of water overnight. Drain, then dry on paper towels. Heat 1 cm *deep sunflower oil* in a deep frying pan. Add the beans and cook for 10–12 minutes, or until medium brown and crisp. Drain on paper towels. Allow to cool. Heat a clean frying pan over medium heat. Add *1 tablespoon sesame seeds* and *1 teaspoon sea salt* and lightly toast for 2–4 minutes, stirring continually. Grind the sesame seed mixture in a spice grinder until fine. Combine the beans and the sesame salt. Store in an airtight container for 3 weeks.

SPICY TEMPEH STICKS

Place *3 cloves coarsley chopped garlic, 4 chopped spring onions, 4 chopped blanched almonds* and *¼ cup (60 ml) water* in a blender and process until almost smooth. Add *1 tablespoon ground coriander, 1 teaspoon salt, ¼ teaspoon pepper* and *¼ teaspoon cayenne pepper* and briefly blend to combine. Transfer to a large bowl, then whisk in *1 tablespoon plain flour*. Cut a *300 g block seasoned tempeh* lengthways into 6 x 2 cm strips, then cut in half lengthways to form large French fry shapes. Fill a deep heavy-based saucepan one third full of *oil* and heat to moderate 180°C (350°F), or until a cube of bread browns in 15 seconds. Coat the tempeh in the batter and fry in batches for 3–4 minutes, or until golden brown and crisp. Remove with a slotted spoon and drain on paper towels. Repeat with the remaining tempeh. Serve while still hot and crisp.

Clockwise from left: Sesame-crusted tofu snacks, Avocado and black bean salsa, Soy bean hummus, bought soy chips, Crunchy spiced soy beans and Spicy tempeh sticks.

SNACKS

FRESH SOY BEAN NIBBLIES
Wash *350 g frozen soy beans in pods*. Fill a large saucepan with water, add *2 teaspoons salt* and *1 cm x 10 cm piece dried kombu*, then bring to the boil. Add the soy beans and cook for 5 minutes. Drain and cool. Serve the pods seasoned with a little *sea salt*.

SOY BEAN DIP WITH SOY AND LINSEED CROSTINI
Cook *200 g frozen soy beans* in *2 cups (500 ml) vegetable stock* for 10–12 minutes. Drain, reserving *¼ cup (60 ml) of the stock*. Mix the beans in a food processor with *1 clove crushed garlic*, *½ cup (30 g) chopped fresh basil*, *1 tablespoon extra virgin olive oil* and the reserved stock, occasionally scraping down the sides, until smooth. Serve warm with soy and linseed bread crostini. Makes 1½ cups. To make the crostini, preheat the oven to moderate 180°C (350°F/Gas 4). Remove the crusts from *6 slices soy and linseed bread*. Cut each slice into 2.5 cm wide fingers. Place on an oven tray and bake for 8 minutes, or until golden. Rub with the cut side of *½ clove garlic* and serve warm with the soy bean dip.

BEAN CURD SUSHI (INARI SUSHI)
Wash *1¼ cups (270 g) short-grain rice* several times until the water runs clear. Drain. Soak the rice in a saucepan with *400 ml water* for 30 minutes. Add a *pinch of salt* and cover with a tea towel stretched under a tight-fitting lid. Bring to the boil, then reduce to very low and simmer for 10 minutes. Remove from the heat and leave, covered, for 15 minutes. Soak *4 large dried shiitake mushrooms* in *1½ cups (375 ml) warm water* for 30 minutes. Drain, reserving the mushroom liquid. Trim the stems and thinly slice the caps. Place *2½ tablespoons rice vinegar*, *1 tablespoon mirin*, *2 tablespoons sugar* and *1½ teaspoons salt* in a small saucepan. Stir over low heat for 2 minutes, or until the sugar has dissolved. Cool to room temperature and stir in *¼ teaspoon sesame oil*. Place the rice in a large bowl and sprinkle one third of the vinegar mixture over the top, then quickly and lightly fold in with a large metal spoon. Repeat until all the vinegar mixture is used. Gently fold in the mushrooms. Cut a slit along one edge of *12 pre-cooked seasoned bean curd sheets (inari)* then gently ease the sheets apart to make a pouch. Moisten your hands with a little of the reserved mushroom liquid, take a handul of rice, shape it into an oval and gently press it inside the bean curd sheets, leaving 1 cm at the top. Fold over the edges like an envelope. Repeat with the remaining sheets and rice. To serve, place cut-side-down on a plate and sprinkle with *2 teaspoons lightly toasted sesame seeds*.

CRISPY TOFU PRAWN BALLS
Peel and devein *400 g raw prawns* and place in a blender with *200 g silken firm tofu*, *½ tablespoon grated fresh ginger*, *1 tablespoon fish sauce*, *½ cup (15 g) coriander leaves* and *3 chopped small fresh red chillies* and blend together well. Transfer to a bowl and stir in *½ cup (50 g) soy flour*. Chill for 30 minutes. To make the dipping sauce, combine *1 tablespoon fish sauce*, *1 tablespoon rice vinegar*, *1 tablespoon lime juice*, *1 tablespoon water*, *½ teaspoon sugar* and *1 tablespoon chopped fresh coriander leaves* and whisk together well. Fill a deep heavy-based saucepan one third full of *oil* and heat to 170°C (325°F), or until a cube of bread browns in 20 seconds. Add rounded teaspoons of the prawn mixture and cook in batches for 3 minutes, or until browned all over. Drain on paper towels. Serve with the dipping sauce. Makes about 25.

Clockwise from left: Fresh soy bean nibblies, Soy bean dip with soy and linseed crostini, Bean curd sushi (inari sushi) and Crispy tofu prawn balls.

SOY BEAN TERRINE

Preparation time: 20 minutes +
  overnight soaking
Total cooking time:
  2 hours 20 minutes
Serves 6–8

1 cup (200 g) dried soy beans
1 tablespoon soy bean oil
1 onion, finely chopped
1 zucchini, grated
1/4 cup (7 g) finely chopped fresh
    flat-leaf parsley
1 teaspoon cayenne pepper
3 eggs, lightly beaten
1/3 cup (90 g) sour cream

1/4 cup (60 ml) lemon juice
2 cups (250 g) grated Cheddar
1/2 cup (50 g) grated Parmesan
purchased tomato relish, to serve

1 Soak the soy beans in a bowl with
plenty of cold water for at least
8 hours, or preferably overnight.
Drain well. Place the soy beans in a
large saucepan and add enough water
to cover the beans. Bring to the boil,
then simmer for 1 hour 30 minutes,
or until tender. Drain.
2 Preheat the oven to moderately
hot 190°C (375°F/Gas 5). Lightly
grease a 22 x 12 cm loaf tin and line
the base and sides with baking paper.
Blend the beans in a food processor
until crumbly.

3 Heat the oil in a large frying pan.
Add the onion and zucchini and cook
over medium heat for 5 minutes, or
until golden. Transfer to a bowl and
allow to cool.
4 Add the parsley, cayenne pepper,
egg, sour cream, lemon juice, cheeses
and soy beans and mix together.
Spoon the mixture into the prepared
tin and press down to flatten the top.
Bake for 45 minutes, or until firm.
Cool completely in the tin, then
carefully invert on a platter. Serve
sliced with the tomato relish and a
side salad, if desired.

NUTRITION PER SERVE (8)
Protein 18 g; Fat 22 g; Carbohydrate 3.5 g;
Dietary Fibre 5.5 g; Cholesterol 100 mg;
1190 kJ (285 cal)

*Line the base and sides of the loaf tin with
baking paper.*

*Blend the cooked soy beans in a food
processor until crumbly.*

*Cook the onion and zucchini in a frying
pan until golden.*

POTATO SALAD WITH CREAMY TOFU MAYONNAISE

Preparation time: 20 minutes
Total cooking time: 15 minutes
Serves 4 (as an accompaniment)

1 kg new season potatoes
300 g silken tofu
2 tablespoons fresh lemon juice
2 teaspoons honey

1 tablespoon light soy sauce
2 teaspoons Dijon mustard
3 tablespoons chopped fresh dill
90 ml olive oil
sprigs of thyme, to garnish

1 Scrub the potatoes clean and leave unpeeled. Place in a large saucepan of salted water and bring to the boil. Simmer for 15 minutes, or until tender. Drain well and cool slightly. Cut the potatoes into 2 cm chunks and place in a bowl.
2 Place the tofu, lemon juice, honey,

soy sauce, mustard and dill in a food processor and blend until smooth. Gradually pour in the oil while the machine is still running. Season with salt and freshly ground black pepper.
3 Pour the mayonnaise over the potato pieces and mix gently until well coated. Serve warm or cold garnished with sprigs of thyme.

NUTRITION PER SERVE
Protein 12 g; Fat 25 g; Carbohydrate 36 g;
Dietary Fibre 4 g; Cholesterol 0 mg;
1755 kJ (420 cal)

Cook the potatoes, then cut into even-sized chunks with a sharp knife.

Blend the tofu, lemon juice, honey, soy sauce, mustard, dill and oil until smooth.

Combine the tofu mayonnaise and potato pieces until well coated.

37

SPICED SOY BEAN PATTIES WITH SALSA

Preparation time: 20 minutes
Total cooking time: 15 minutes
Serves 4

Salsa
1 cucumber, seeded and diced
1 tomato, seeded and diced
1/4 red onion, finely chopped
1 tablespoon chopped fresh coriander
   leaves
1 tablespoon chopped fresh mint
2 tablespoons olive oil
1 tablespoon white wine vinegar

Patties
1/2 teaspoon finely grated lemon rind
1 tablespoon lemon juice
2 x 300 g cans soy beans, rinsed
   and drained
1/3 cup (10 g) roughly chopped fresh
   flat-leaf parsley
3/4 cup (60 g) fresh breadcrumbs
2 teaspoons ground cumin
2 teaspoons ground coriander
3/4 teaspoon paprika
2 tablespoons soy bean oil
4 slices crusty bread, toasted

1 Combine the salsa ingredients in a bowl and stir together well. Season.
2 Place the lemon rind, lemon juice, soy beans and parsley in a food processor and blend in bursts until roughly mashed. Transfer to a large bowl and add the breadcrumbs, ground cumin, ground coriander and paprika and mix together well. Divide the mixture into four portions using damp hands. Shape into patties 8 cm in diameter.
3 Heat the oil in a large frying pan over medium heat, add the patties in batches and cook on each side for 3 minutes, or until golden brown.
4 Serve the patties with crusty bread, topped with salsa.

NUTRITION PER SERVE
Protein 18 g; Fat 30 g; Carbohydrate 28 g;
Dietary Fibre 10 g; Cholesterol 0 mg;
1855 kJ (443 cal)

Remove the seeds from the cucumber by scraping downward with a spoon.

Roughly process the soy beans, parsley, lemon rind and lemon juice.

Shape the soy bean mixture into patties using damp hands.

MARINATED GRILLED TOFU SALAD WITH GINGER MISO DRESSING

Preparation time: 20 minutes +
 overnight marinating
Total cooking time: 5 minutes
Serves 4

1/3 cup (80 ml) tamari, shoyu or
 light soy sauce
2 teaspoons soy bean oil
2 cloves garlic, crushed
1 teaspoon grated fresh ginger
1 teaspoon chilli paste
500 g firm tofu, cut into 2 cm cubes
400 g mesclun leaves
1 Lebanese cucumber, finely sliced
250 g cherry tomatoes, halved
2 teaspoons soy bean oil, extra

Dressing
2 teaspoons white miso paste
2 tablespoons mirin
1 teaspoon sesame oil
1 teaspoon grated fresh ginger
1 teaspoon finely chopped chives
1 tablespoon toasted sesame seeds

1 Mix together the tamari, soy bean oil, garlic, ginger, chilli paste and 1/2 teaspoon salt in a bowl. Add the tofu and mix until well coated. Marinate for at least 10 minutes, or preferably overnight. Drain and reserve the marinade.

2 To make the dressing, combine the miso with 1/2 cup (125 ml) hot water and leave until the miso dissolves. Add the mirin, sesame oil, ginger, chives and sesame seeds and stir thoroughly until it begins to thicken.

3 Combine the mesclun leaves, cucumber and tomato in a serving bowl and leave until ready to serve.

4 Heat the extra soy bean oil on a chargrill or hotplate. Add the tofu and cook over medium heat for 4 minutes, or until golden brown. Pour on the reserved marinade and cook for a further 1 minute over high heat. Remove from the grill and allow to cool for 5 minutes.

5 Add the tofu to the salad, drizzle with the dressing and toss well.

NUTRITION PER SERVE
Protein 12 g; Fat 8 g; Carbohydrate 4 g;
Dietary Fibre 4 g; Cholesterol 0 mg;
590 kJ (140 cal)

COOK'S FILE
Note: Miso is Japanese bean paste and plays an important part in their cuisine. It is commonly used in soups, dressings, on grilled foods and as a flavouring for pickles.

Gently stir the tofu cubes through the marinade until well coated.

Stir the dressing ingredients together until it begins to thicken.

Cook the tofu cubes over medium heat until each side is golden brown.

39

VEGETARIAN MAIN MEALS

INDIVIDUAL TEMPEH LASAGNE

Preparation time: 25 minutes
Total cooking time: 40 minutes
Serves 6

4 tablespoons olive oil
1 onion, chopped
3 cloves garlic, chopped
600 g bottled tomato pasta sauce
1/2 cup (80 g) sun-dried tomatoes,
    drained and finely sliced
1/4 cup (60 ml) dry white wine
1 tablespoon shredded fresh basil
2 x 300 g blocks tempeh,
    cut lengthways into 3 thin slices,
    then halved
120 g baby spinach leaves
1 teaspoon chopped garlic, extra
3 cups (450 g) grated mozarella
fresh basil leaves, to garnish

1 Preheat the oven to moderate 180°C (350°F/Gas 4).
2 Heat 1 tablespoon of the oil in a saucepan. Add the onion and garlic and gently cook over medium heat for 5 minutes, or until the onion is lightly golden. Add the bottled pasta sauce, sun-dried tomato and white wine. Season with salt and freshly ground black pepper. Cook for 20 minutes, or until thick and pulpy. Cool slightly, then stir in the basil.
3 Heat the remaining oil in a frying pan. Add the tempeh slices and cook for 5–8 minutes, or until crisp and golden. Drain on paper towels. Add the baby spinach to the same frying pan with the extra garlic and 1 tablespoon water, and cook until the spinach has wilted. Set aside.
4 Place a slice of tempeh on the bottom of 6 individual gratin dishes. Cover with a little tomato sauce, some spinach and half of the mozzarella. Repeat with another layer of tempeh, sauce, spinach and the remaining mozzarella. Bake for 10–15 minutes, or until golden brown. Garnish with fresh basil leaves and serve with a fresh green salad, if desired.

NUTRITION PER SERVE
Protein 130 g; Fat 34 g; Carbohydrate 10 g;
Dietary Fibre 3 g; Cholesterol 47 mg;
1975 kJ (470 cal)

COOK'S FILE
Note: If you don't have individual gratin dishes, build each lasagne free-form style on a large baking tray. Once cooked, carefully transfer to serving plates with a spatula.

Cook the tomato sauce until it reaches a thick and pulpy consistency.

Shallow-fry the slices of tempeh until crisp and golden on both sides.

TOFU KEBABS WITH ASIAN MISO PESTO

Preparation time: 30 minutes +
  1 hour marinating
Total cooking time: 10 minutes
Serves 4

1 large red capsicum, cut into squares
12 button mushrooms, halved
6 pickling onions, quartered
3 zucchini, cut into 3 cm chunks
450 g firm tofu, cut into 2 cm cubes
1/2 cup (125 ml) light olive oil
1/4 cup (60 ml) light soy sauce
2 cloves garlic, crushed
2 teaspoons grated fresh ginger

Miso pesto
1/2 cup (80 g) unsalted roasted
  peanuts
2 cups (60 g) firmly packed fresh
  coriander leaves
2 tablespoons white miso paste
2 cloves garlic
100 ml olive oil

1 Soak 12 wooden skewers in cold water for 10 minutes. Thread the vegetable pieces and tofu alternately onto the skewers, then place in a large rectangular ceramic dish.
2 Combine the olive oil, soy sauce, garlic and ginger in a bowl, then pour half the mixture over the kebabs. Cover with plastic wrap and marinate for 1 hour.

3 To make the miso pesto, finely chop the peanuts, coriander leaves, miso paste and garlic in a food processor. Slowly add the olive oil while the machine is still running and blend until a smooth paste.
4 Heat a grill plate and cook the kebabs, turning and brushing frequently with the remaining marinade, for 4–6 minutes, or until the edges are slightly brown. Serve with steamed rice and a little of the miso pesto.

NUTRITION PER SERVE
Protein 8 g; Fat 64 g; Carbohydrate 10 g;
Dietary Fibre 4 g; Cholesterol 0 mg;
2698 kJ (645 cal)

Thread the vegetable pieces and tofu cubes alternately onto the skewers.

Mix the nuts, coriander leaves, miso and garlic until finely chopped.

Brush the kebabs with the remaining marinade during cooking.

TOFU WITH ASIAN GREENS AND SHIITAKE MUSHROOMS

Preparation time: 15 minutes
Total cooking time: 20 minutes
Serves 4

1/3 cup (80 ml) vegetable oil
1 clove garlic, chopped
1 teaspoon grated fresh ginger
60 g shiitake mushrooms, sliced
2 teaspoons dashi powder
3 tablespoons mushroom soy sauce
3 tablespoons mirin
1 teaspoon sugar
2 tablespoons cornflour
2 x 300 g silken firm tofu, each block
   cut into 4 slices
250 g bok choy, chopped
150 g choy sum, chopped
2 spring onions, cut on the diagonal
wasabi, to serve

1 Heat 1 tablespoon of the oil in a saucepan. Add the garlic, ginger and mushrooms and fry for 1–2 minutes, or until softened. Add the dashi powder and 2 cups (500 ml) water. Bring to the boil, reduce the heat and simmer for 5 minutes.

2 Add the mushroom soy sauce, mirin and sugar and stir until the sugar has dissolved. Combine the cornflour with a little water in a small bowl to make a smooth paste. Pour into the soy sauce mixture and stir until thickened.

3 Heat 2 tablespoons of the oil in a frying pan. Add the tofu and cook in batches for 2–3 minutes, or until brown on both sides. Set aside and keep warm. Heat the remaining oil, then add the bok choy, choy sum and spring onion. Cook for 2 minutes, or until the greens are wilted.

4 Place the greens in a bowl, top with the tofu and pour on the dashi sauce. Serve with rice and a little wasabi on the side.

NUTRITION PER SERVE
Protein 17 g; Fat 25 g; Carbohydrate 6 g; Dietary Fibre 5 g; Cholesterol 0 mg; 1368 kJ (327 cal)

Stir the cornflour paste into the liquid until it thickens.

Fry the slices of tofu in hot oil until brown on both sides.

TOFU FAJITAS

Preparation time: 25 minutes
Total cooking time: 20 minutes
Serves 4

4 tablespoons light soy sauce
2 cloves garlic, crushed
400 g smoked tofu, cut into 5 cm
    strips
200 g canned tomatoes
1 small onion, roughly chopped
1 small fresh red chilli, seeded and
    finely chopped
3 tablespoons chopped fresh
    coriander leaves
1 large ripe avocado
2 teaspoons lemon juice
1 cup (250 g) sour cream
2 tablespoons soy bean oil
1 red capsicum, seeded and sliced
1 yellow capsicum, seeded and sliced
8 spring onions, cut into 5 cm lengths
8 large (15 cm) flour tortillas

1 Place the soy sauce, garlic and 1 teaspoon freshly ground black pepper in a shallow ceramic dish. Add the tofu and toss together well. Cover and leave to marinate.
2 Combine the tomatoes, onion, chilli and coriander in a food processor until smooth. Season with salt and freshly ground black pepper. Transfer to a small saucepan, and bring to the boil. Reduce the heat and simmer for 10 minutes. Cool.
3 Halve the avocado, then remove the stone. Scoop the flesh into a bowl and add the lemon juice and 2 tablespoons of the sour cream. Season with salt and freshly ground black pepper. Mash well with a fork.
4 Heat 1 tablespoon oil in a frying pan. Add the tofu and any remaining marinade and cook, stirring, over high heat for 4–5 minutes. Remove from the pan. Heat the remaining oil in the pan. Add the red and yellow capsicum and spring onion, season with salt and freshly ground black pepper and cook for 3–4 minutes.
5 Cook the tortillas quickly in a dry clean frying pan over high heat for 5 seconds on each side.
6 To serve, spread a tortilla with a little avocado mixture, tomato salsa and sour cream. Top with some tofu and vegetables, fold in one end and roll. Repeat with the remaining tortillas and fillings.

NUTRITION PER SERVE
Protein 19 g; Fat 45 g; Carbohydrate 87 g; Dietary Fibre 7 g; Cholesterol 82 mg; 3464 kJ (828 cal)

Blend the tomatoes, onion, chilli and coriander until smooth.

Remove the stone and scoop the avocado flesh into a bowl.

Roll up the filled tortilla, tucking in one end as you go, to encase the filling.

SWEET AND SOUR TOFU

Preparation time: 15 minutes
Total cooking time: 20 minutes
Serves 4

600 g firm tofu
3–4 tablespoons soy bean oil
1 large carrot, julienned
2 cups (150 g) trimmed bean sprouts
  or soy bean sprouts
1 cup (95 g) sliced button mushrooms
6–8 spring onions, cut diagonally
100 g snow peas, cut in half on the
  diagonal

1/3 cup (80 ml) rice vinegar
2 tablespoons light soy sauce
1 1/2 tablespoons caster sugar
2 tablespoons tomato sauce
1 1/2 cups (375 ml) chicken or
  vegetable stock
1 tablespoon cornflour

1 Cut the tofu in half horizontally, then cut into 16 triangles in total. Heat 2 tablespoons of the oil in a frying pan. Add the tofu in batches and cook over medium heat for 2 minutes on each side, or until crisp and golden. Drain on paper towels. Keep warm.
2 Wipe the pan clean and heat the remaining oil. Add the carrot, bean sprouts, mushrooms, spring onion and snow peas and stir-fry for 1 minute. Add the vinegar, soy sauce, sugar, tomato sauce and stock and cook for a further 1 minute.
3 Combine the cornflour with 2 tablespoons water. Add to the vegetable mixture and cook until the sauce thickens. Divide the tofu among the serving bowls and spoon some sauce over the top. Serve with steamed rice on the side.

NUTRITION PER SERVE
Protein 15 g; Fat 16 g; Carbohydrate 17 g; Dietary Fibre 4 g; Cholesterol 0 mg; 1178 kJ (280 cal)

Cut the tofu slices into triangles with a sharp knife.

Fry the tofu triangles on both sides until crisp and golden.

Stir the sauce and vegetables together until the sauce thickens.

SHIITAKE MUSHROOM AND FRESH SOY BEAN RISOTTO

Preparation time: 15 minutes +
20 minutes soaking
Total cooking time: 40 minutes
Serves 4

10 g dried shiitake mushrooms, sliced
1 cup (160 g) frozen soy beans
3 cups (750 ml) vegetable stock
3 tablespoons soy spread or
  margarine
1 onion, finely diced
1 cup (220 g) arborio rice

1/2 cup (125 ml) white wine
1/2 teaspoon ground white pepper
1/2 cup (50 g) grated fresh Parmesan
1 tablespoon chopped fresh parsley

1 Soak the shiitake mushrooms in
1 cup (250 ml) warm water for
20 minutes. Drain and reserve the
liquid. Cook the soy beans in a
saucepan of boiling water for
2 minutes. Drain. Place the stock
and reserved mushroom liquid in
a saucepan and keep at a low simmer.
2 Melt the soy spread in a saucepan.
Add the onion and cook over low
heat for 5 minutes, or until soft.
Increase the heat to medium, add
the rice and stir to coat. Pour in the

wine and season with salt and white
pepper. Cook for a further 2 minutes,
or until the wine has been absorbed.
3 Add 1/4 cup (60 ml) of the hot
liquid and stir constantly. Continue
adding the liquid, 1/4 cup (60 ml) at a
time, stirring constantly, and cook for
20–25 minutes, or until the liquid
has been absorbed after each addition.
With the last 1/4 cup (60 ml) liquid,
add the soy beans and mushrooms
and cook for a further 2 minutes. Stir
in the Parmesan and serve garnished
with the parsley.

NUTRITION PER SERVE
Protein 22 g; Fat 13 g; Carbohydrate 48 g;
Dietary Fibre 10 g; Cholesterol 12 mg;
1742 kJ (416 cal)

*Cook the onion in the melted soy spread
until the onion is soft.*

*Stir the rice and wine over medium heat
until the wine has been absorbed.*

*Add the hot liquid 1/4 cup (60 ml) at a time,
stirring constantly.*

SOY PASTA WITH MEDITERRANEAN VEGETABLES AND TOFU

Preparation time: 25 minutes
Total cooking time: 15 minutes
Serves 4–6

300 g firm tofu, cut into 1 cm cubes
100 ml extra virgin olive oil
1 tablespoon finely chopped fresh basil
1 tablespoon finely chopped fresh oregano
2 large cloves garlic, finely chopped

1 red onion, thinly sliced
250 g soy pasta
2 tablespoons olive oil
1 eggplant, cut into 2 cm cubes
1 zucchini, cut into 1 cm slices
6 tomatoes, seeded and diced
70 g whole pitted Kalamata olives
fresh basil, to serve

1 Place the tofu in a large bowl. Add the extra virgin olive oil, basil, oregano, garlic, onion, 2 teaspoons salt and 1 teaspoon pepper. Stir to coat and set aside.

2 Cook the pasta in a large saucepan of boiling water for 10 minutes, or until *al dente*. Keep warm.

3 Meanwhile, heat the olive oil in a large frying pan. Add the eggplant and cook over medium heat for 4 minutes. Season to taste with salt and freshly ground black pepper. Add the zucchini and cook for a further 6 minutes. Add the tomato and cook for 1 minute, or until warmed through.

4 Add the tofu mixture to the pan and heat through. Combine with the olives and pasta and serve, garnished with basil.

NUTRITION PER SERVE (6)
Protein 11 g; Fat 19 g; Carbohydrate 35 g;
Dietary Fibre 6 g; Cholesterol 0 mg;
1502 kJ (359 cal)

Remove the seeds from the tomatoes and dice the flesh.

Cook the eggplant and the zucchini until browned on all sides.

Add the tomato to the vegetables and cook for another minute.

BEER-BATTERED TEMPEH WITH WEDGES AND AVOCADO AIOLI

Preparation time: 20 minutes
Total cooking time: 40 minutes
Serves 4

4 potatoes (600 g), each cut into
   8 wedges
2 tablespoons soy bean oil
1/2 cup (55 g) besan (chickpea flour)
2 tablespoons soy flour
2 tablespoons cumin seeds, toasted
   and ground
2 tablespoons coriander seeds,
   toasted and ground
1 tablespoon sweet paprika powder
2/3 cup (170 ml) beer
vegetable oil, for deep-frying
600 g tempeh, cut into 12 fingers
   (10 x 2 cm)
fresh coriander leaves, to garnish,
   optional
spring onions, sliced, to garnish,
   optional

Avocado aïoli
1/2 cup (15 g) fresh coriander leaves
1 clove garlic, crushed
1/4 cup (60 ml) extra virgin olive oil
1/2 teaspoon chilli flakes
2 teaspoons lemon juice
1 fresh jalapeño chilli, finely chopped
1 medium or 1/2 large avocado,
   chopped

1 Preheat the oven to moderate 180°C (350°F/Gas 4). Place the potato wedges on a baking tray, drizzle with the soy bean oil and season with salt and pepper. Toss to coat well. Bake for 40 minutes, or until golden brown.

2 Meanwhile, to make the avocado aïoli, combine the coriander leaves, garlic, oil, chilli flakes, lemon juice, chilli, avocado and 1 teaspoon salt in a food processor until smooth. Set aside until ready to serve.
3 Place the chickpea and soy flours, cumin, coriander, paprika, beer and 1 teaspoon salt in a bowl and mix to a medium thick batter.
4 Fill a deep heavy-based saucepan one third full with oil and heat to 170°C (325°F), or until a cube of bread browns in 20 seconds. Dip the slices of tempeh in the batter, then deep-fry in batches for 1 minute, or until golden. Drain on crumpled paper towels.
5 Serve the tempeh with the wedges and aïoli on the side. Garnish with the coriander leaves and spring onion, if desired.

NUTRITION PER SERVE
Protein 20 g; Fat 27 g; Carbohydrate 30 g;
Dietary Fibre 5 g; Cholesterol 0 mg;
1937 kJ (463 cal)

Toss the potato wedges and soy bean oil together and season.

Dip the tempeh slices in the thick beer batter.

Deep-fry the tempeh until golden, then remove with a slotted spoon.

TOFU AND SPINACH CANNELLONI WITH FRESH TOMATO SAUCE

Preparation time: 50 minutes
Total cooking time:
  1 hour 15 minutes
Serves 6–8

2 tablespoons soy bean oil
1 onion, chopped
2 cloves garlic, crushed
1/4 cup (60 g) tomato paste
950 g tomatoes, seeded and diced
1 teaspoon sugar
1 1/2 cups (375 ml) vegetable stock
1 tablespoon finely chopped fresh
  basil
1 tablespoon finely chopped fresh
  oregano
270 g cannelloni tubes
grated Parmesan, to garnish

Filling
300 g chopped fresh English spinach
500 g firm tofu, mashed
3/4 cup (75 g) grated Parmesan
1/2 cup (80 g) pine nuts, toasted

Béchamel
3 tablespoons soy spread or
  margarine
5 tablespoons plain flour
1 litre malt-free soy milk
1/2 teaspoon ground nutmeg

1 Preheat the oven to moderately hot 200°C (400°F/Gas 6). Heat the oil in a saucepan over medium heat. Add the onion and garlic, cook for 3 minutes, then stir in the tomato paste. Cook for 2 minutes. Add the tomato and sugar and cook, stirring frequently, for 4 minutes. Gradually add the stock and bring to the boil, then simmer for 25 minutes, or until thickened. Remove from the heat and stir in the basil and oregano.
2 To make the filling, steam the spinach for 3 minutes, or until wilted. Allow to cool, then squeeze out any excess water. Combine the spinach, tofu, Parmesan and half the pine nuts in a bowl. Season with salt and black pepper.
3 To make the béchamel, melt the soy spread in a saucepan. Add the flour and cook, stirring constantly, over medium heat for 2 minutes. Reduce the heat and gradually whisk in the milk. Add the nutmeg and season to taste. Simmer, stirring constantly, for 5 minutes, or until the sauce thickens.
4 Pour half the tomato sauce and half the béchamel over the base of a large rectangular 30 x 21 x 5 cm ovenproof dish. Spoon the tofu filling into the cannelloni tubes and arrange in the dish. Pour the remaining tomato sauce over the cannelloni, followed by the béchamel, then sprinkle the remaining pine nuts on top. Bake for 30 minutes, or until bubbling and lightly golden. Garnish with grated Parmesan.

NUTRITION PER SERVE (8)
Protein 23 g; Fat 30 g; Carbohydrate 51 g; Dietary Fibre 9 g; Cholesterol 9 mg; 2254 kJ (538 cal)

Cook the tomato mixture until the sauce thickens and becomes pulpy.

Squeeze the excess water from the spinach leaves.

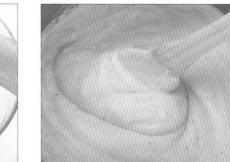

Constantly stir the béchamel until the sauce thickens.

TOFU IN BLACK BEAN SAUCE

Preparation time: 20 minutes
Total cooking time: 15 minutes
Serves 4

⅓ cup (80 ml) vegetable stock
2 teaspoons cornflour
2 teaspoons Chinese rice wine
1 teaspoon sesame oil
1 tablespoon soy sauce
2 tablespoons peanut oil
450 g firm tofu, cut into 2 cm cubes
2 cloves garlic, very finely chopped
2 teaspoons finely chopped fresh
  ginger
3 tablespoons fermented black
  beans, rinsed and very finely
  chopped
4 spring onions, cut on the diagonal
  (white and green parts)
1 red capsicum, cut into 2 cm chunks
300 g baby bok choy, chopped
  crossways into 2 cm pieces

1 Combine the vegetable stock, cornflour, Chinese rice wine, sesame oil, soy sauce, ½ teaspoon salt and freshly ground black pepper in a small bowl.
2 Heat a wok over medium heat, add the peanut oil and swirl to coat. Add the tofu and stir-fry in two batches for 3 minutes each batch, or until lightly browned. Remove with a slotted spoon and drain on paper towels. Discard any bits of tofu stuck to the wok or floating in the oil.
3 Add the garlic and ginger and stir-fry for 30 seconds. Toss in the black beans and spring onion and stir-fry for 30 seconds. Add the capsicum and stir-fry for 1 minute. Add the bok choy and stir-fry for a further 2 minutes. Return the tofu to the wok and stir gently. Pour in the sauce and stir gently for 2–3 minutes, or until the sauce has thickened slightly. Serve immediately with steamed rice.

NUTRITION PER SERVE
Protein 13 g; Fat 14 g; Carbohydrate 4 g; Dietary Fibre 4 g; Cholesterol 0 mg; 850 kJ (205 cal)

COOK'S FILE
Note: Chinese rice wine is an alcoholic liquid made from cooked glutinous rice and millet mash which has been fermented with yeast, then aged for a period of 10 to 100 years. With a sherry-like taste, it is used as both a drink and a cooking liquid.

Stir-fry the tofu cubes in batches until lightly brown.

Stir-fry the garlic, ginger, black beans and spring onion.

Return the tofu to the wok and gently stir together with the vegetables.

TEMPEH & MUSHROOM LOAF WITH GARLIC MASH

Preparation time: 40 minutes
Total cooking time: 50 minutes
Serves 4

1 tablespoon soy bean oil
1 onion, finely chopped
250 g field mushrooms, finely
    chopped
1 cup (155 g) brazil nuts, roasted
1 cup (155 g) unsalted roasted
    cashews
300 g seasoned tempeh, roughly
    chopped
1½ cups (120 g) fresh breadcrumbs
100 g onion and garlic flavoured soy
    cheese, grated
¼ teaspoon dried mixed herbs
1 egg, lightly beaten

Garlic mash

1 kg potatoes, peeled and chopped
2 cups (500 ml) vegetable stock
1 clove garlic, crushed
1 teaspoon butter
2 tablespoons cream

Tomato sauce

1 tablespoon soy bean oil
1 small onion, finely chopped
1 clove garlic
400 g can chopped tomatoes
1–2 teaspoons sugar
2 teaspoons balsamic vinegar
1 teaspoon chopped fresh oregano

1 Preheat the oven to moderate 180°C (350°F/Gas 4). Grease a 10 x 22 cm loaf tin and line the base with baking paper. Heat the oil in a large frying pan. Add the onion and mushrooms and cook for 5 minutes, or until soft and the liquid has evaporated. Cool.

2 Grind the brazil nuts and cashews in a food processor for 10–15 seconds—ensure they are not too finely ground. Transfer to a large bowl. Process the tempeh for 15 seconds, or until coarsely ground. Add to the nuts, along with the mushroom mixture, breadcrumbs, soy cheese, mixed herbs and egg. Season with salt and freshly ground black pepper. Mix together with your hands until well combined. Spoon into the prepared tin and press down on the surface. Bake for 45 minutes, or until firm.

3 Meanwhile, to make the garlic mash, place the potato in a large saucepan. Add the stock and enough water to cover—about 1 cup (250 ml). Bring to the boil, then reduce the heat and simmer for 15–20 minutes, or until soft. Drain, reserving ⅓ cup (80 ml) of the cooking liquid. Mash the potato, then mix in the garlic, butter, cream and the reserved cooking liquid. Season with salt and white pepper.

4 To make the sauce, heat the oil in a saucepan. Add the onion and cook over medium heat for 2 minutes, or until soft—do not brown. Add the garlic and cook for 1 minute. Add the tomatoes with any liquid and bring to the boil. Reduce the heat, add the sugar and vinegar and simmer for 8–10 minutes, or until reduced and thickened. Add the chopped oregano and simmer for another 2 minutes.

5 Slice the tempeh loaf and serve with the sauce and a dollop of mash on the side.

NUTRITION PER SERVE
Protein 40 g; Fat 85 g; Carbohydrate 77 g; Dietary Fibre 17 g; Cholesterol 62 mg; 5195 kJ (1240 cal)

Cook the onion and mushrooms until soft and the liquid has evaporated.

Mix together the loaf ingredients with your hands until well combined.

PEANUT AND LIME-CRUSTED TOFU WITH CHILLI JAM

Preparation time: 15 minutes
Total cooking time: 15 minutes
Serves 4

¼ cup (30 g) besan (chickpea flour)
2 tablespoons soy flour
2 tablespoons soy sauce
2 tablespóons peanut butter
1 fresh kaffir lime leaf, finely shredded
peanut oil, for deep-frying
500 g firm tofu, cut into 2 cm slices
600 g bok choy, quartered lengthways
1 tablespoon purchased chilli jam
fresh kaffir lime leaf, shredded, extra,
    to garnish

1 Combine the besan and soy flours, soy sauce, peanut butter, shredded lime leaf and 2 teaspoons salt in a bowl. Slowly add 100 ml water, stirring constantly, until the batter reaches a medium thick consistency.
2 Fill a large heavy-based deep saucepan one third full of oil and heat to 190°C (375°F), or until a cube of bread browns in 10 seconds. Quickly dip 2–3 slices of the tofu in the batter and deep-fry for 2 minutes, or until golden brown. Drain on paper towels and keep warm while you repeat with the remaining tofu slices and batter.
3 Steam the bok choy in a saucepan for 2–3 minutes, or until tender but still bright green. Divide the greens among the serving plates, arrange three pieces of tofu on top, dollop with a teaspoon of chilli jam and garnish with the extra shredded kaffir lime leaf.

NUTRITION PER SERVE
Protein 24 g; Fat 24 g; Carbohydrate 8.5 g; Dietary Fibre 9.5 g; Cholesterol 0 mg; 1465 kJ (350 cal)

COOK'S FILE
Note: To make a quick chilli jam, soak 10 dried long red chillies in a bowl of boiling water for 15 minutes. Drain, then remove the seeds and chop. Place in a food processor, then add 4 tablespoons peanut oil, 1 chopped red capsicum, 1 peeled and roughly chopped head (50 g) garlic and 200 g chopped red Asian shallots and blend until smooth. Heat a wok over medium heat and add the chilli mixture. Cook, stirring occasionally, for 15 minutes. Add 2 tablespoons tamarind purée and 100 g grated palm sugar and simmer for 10 minutes, or until it darkens and reaches a jam-like consistency.

Cut the kaffir lime leaf into fine shreds using a sharp knife.

Dip each slice of tofu into the batter until well coated.

Deep-fry the battered tofu until golden brown, then remove with a slotted spoon.

TOFU STROGANOFF

Preparation time: 20 minutes
Total cooking time: 30 minutes
Serves 4

2 tablespoons plain flour
1 tablespoon paprika
500 g firm tofu, cut into 1.5 cm cubes
1 tablespoon soy bean oil
2 teaspoons tomato paste
¼ cup (60 ml) dry sherry
2 cups (500 ml) vegetable stock
12 pickling onions, halved
1 clove garlic, crushed
225 g field mushrooms, cut into
    1 cm slices
3 tablespoons sour cream
sour cream, extra, to garnish
2 tablespoons chopped fresh chives

1 Place the flour and paprika in a plastic bag and season well with salt and freshly ground black pepper. Add the tofu and shake well to coat.
2 Heat the soy bean oil in a frying pan. Add the tofu and cook over medium heat for 4 minutes, or until golden all over. Add the tomato paste and cook for a further 1 minute. Pour in 2 tablespoons of the sherry, cook for 30 seconds then transfer to a bowl. Keep any remaining flour in the pan—do not wipe clean.
3 Pour 1 cup (250 ml) of the stock into the pan and bring to the boil. Add the onion, garlic and mushrooms, reduce the heat to medium and simmer, covered, for 10 minutes.
4 Return the tofu to the pan with the remaining sherry and remaining stock. Season to taste with salt and freshly ground black pepper. Return to the boil, reduce the heat and

simmer for 5 minutes, or until heated through and the sauce has thickened.
5 Remove the pan from the heat and stir a little of the sauce into the sour cream until smooth and of pouring consistency. Pour the sour cream mixture back into the pan—this technique prevents the sour cream from separating and will give the sauce a smoother consistency.

6 Garnish with a dollop of the extra sour cream and sprinkle with the chopped chives. Serve with noodles or steamed rice.

NUTRITION PER SERVE
Protein 12 g; Fat 16 g; Carbohydrate 13 g; Dietary Fibre 2.5 g; Cholesterol 20 mg; 1142 kJ (273 cal)

Shake the tofu in the seasoned flour and paprika until well coated.

Cook the browned tofu with the tomato paste and sherry, then transfer to a bowl.

Simmer the stroganoff until the sauce has thickened and heated through.

MEDITERRANEAN PIZZA

Preparation time: 35 minutes +
    35 minutes rising
Total cooking time: 25 minutes
Serves 4

7 g sachet dried yeast
1 teaspoon sugar
2¼ cups (280 g) plain flour
½ cup (50 g) soy flour
soy oil, for greasing
1½ tablespoons purchased sun-dried
    tomato pesto
100 g soy cheese, grated
⅓ cup (40 g) grated Cheddar
1 small red capsicum, thinly sliced
½ red onion, thinly sliced
2 tablespoons pine nuts
10 pitted black olives
fresh basil, to garnish

1 To make the pizza base, place the
yeast, sugar, ½ teaspoon salt and
1 cup (250 ml) warm water in a bowl
and stir until dissolved. Cover with
plastic wrap and leave in a warm
place for 10 minutes, or until bubbles
appear on the surface. The mixture
should be frothy and slightly
increased in volume. If your yeast
doesn't foam it is dead, so you will
have to discard it and start again.
2 Sift the plain and soy flours into a
large bowl. Make a well in the centre
and add the yeast mixture. Mix to
form a dough. Knead the dough on a
lightly floured surface for 10 minutes,
or until smooth and elastic. Cover
and set aside in a warm place for
25 minutes, or until doubled in size.
3 Preheat the oven to moderately
hot 200°C (400°F/Gas 6). Grease a
30 cm pizza tray with the soy oil.

Roll out the dough on a lightly
floured surface to a 34 cm circle,
transfer to the prepared tray, fold
over the edge and press down.
4 Spread the base with the sun-dried
tomato pesto and sprinkle with the
combined soy and Cheddar cheeses.
Top with the capsicum, onion, pine
nuts and olives. Season to taste with
freshly ground black pepper. Bake

for 20–25 minutes, or until golden
brown and cooked through.
5 Garnish with the fresh basil leaves
and cut into wedges to serve.

NUTRITION PER SERVE
Protein 23 g; Fat 20 g; Carbohydrate 57 g;
Dietary Fibre 6 g; Cholesterol 0 mg;
2108 kJ (504 cal)

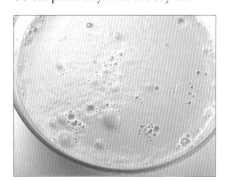

*Leave the yeast until bubbles appear and
the mixture is frothy.*

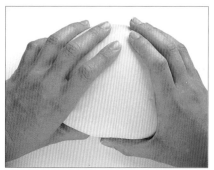

*Knead the dough until smooth and elastic,
then form into a ball.*

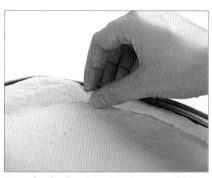

*Transfer the dough to the pizza tray, fold
down the edge and press down.*

Cook the onion, garlic and celery until they are softened.

Cook the eggplant and celery mixture until the eggplant is tender.

Spoon the vegetable and soy bean filling into the eggplant shells.

EGGPLANT STUFFED WITH SOY BEANS AND VEGETABLES

Preparation time: 30 minutes
Total cooking time:
    1 hour 35 minutes
Serves 4

2 x 350 g eggplants
2 tablespoons soy bean oil
1 onion, chopped
2 cloves garlic, crushed
1 celery stick, finely chopped
415 g can diced tomatoes
1 1/2 tablespoons tomato paste
1/2 cup (125 ml) white wine
3/4 cup (185 ml) vegetable stock
    or water
300 g can soy beans, rinsed and
    drained
1/2 teaspoon sugar
3/4 cup (45 g) chopped fresh parsley
100 g soy cheese, grated
3/4 cup (75 g) coarsely grated
    Parmesan

1 Preheat the oven to moderate 180°C (350°F/Gas 4). Pour 1/2 cup (125 ml) water into an ovenproof ceramic dish. Halve the eggplants lengthways and scoop out the flesh with a spoon leaving a 1 cm border. Dice the flesh. Arrange the shells in the prepared dish.
2 Heat the oil in a large frying pan. Add the onion, garlic and celery and cook over medium heat for 5 minutes, or until softened. Add the diced eggplant flesh and cook, stirring frequently, for a further 10 minutes, or until the eggplant is tender. Add the tomato, tomato paste, wine and stock and cook, stirring, for 8 minutes, or until reduced slightly. Season with salt and pepper. Add the soy beans, sugar and 1/2 cup (30 g) of the parsley and cook for a further 5 minutes. Remove from the heat and stir through the soy cheese and 1/2 cup (50 g) of the Parmesan.
3 Pack the filling into the eggplant shells with a spoon. Use pieces of foil to prop up the outer walls if necessary. Cover loosely with foil. Bake for 1 hour, or until the flesh of the eggplant shell is cooked.
4 Remove the foil and sprinkle with the remaining Parmesan. Cook under a hot grill for 2–3 minutes, or until golden. Sprinkle with the remaining parsley and serve hot.

NUTRITION PER SERVE
Protein 24 g; Fat 30 g; Carbohydrate 13 g;
Dietary Fibre 10 g; Cholesterol 0 mg;
1794 kJ (430 cal)

SOY BEAN ENCHILADAS

Preparation time: 35 minutes
Total cooking time: 1 hour
Serves 4

Sauce
2 teaspoons soy bean oil
1 onion, finely chopped
2 cloves garlic, crushed
1 teaspoon ground cumin
1 teaspoon ground coriander
1/2 teaspoon chilli powder
400 g can puréed tomato
1/2 cup (125 ml) vegetable stock
1 teaspoon sugar

550 g butternut pumpkin, peeled
   and seeded
2 teaspoons soy bean oil
1 onion, finely chopped
1 teaspoon chilli powder
425 g can diced tomato
300 g can soy beans, rinsed and
   drained
200 g can corn kernels, drained
8 large corn tortillas
100 g soy cheese, grated
fresh parsley, chopped, to garnish

1 Preheat the oven to moderate
180°C (350°F/Gas 4). Grease a 22 x
32 x 6 cm ovenproof ceramic dish.
2 To make the sauce, heat the oil in
a saucepan. Add the onion and cook
over medium heat for 3 minutes, or
until soft. Add the garlic, ground
cumin, ground coriander and chilli
powder. Cook, stirring, for 1 minute.
Stir in the puréed tomato and stock
and bring to the boil. Reduce the
heat and simmer for 5 minutes. Add
the sugar and season with salt and
freshly ground black pepper.

3 To make the filling, cut the
pumpkin into 1.5 cm cubes. Steam
for 12 minutes, or until just tender.
Heat the oil in a saucepan, add the
onion and cook over medium heat
for 3 minutes, or until soft. Add the
chilli powder, cook for 30 seconds,
then add the tomato and simmer
for 15 minutes, or until pulpy. Add
the pumpkin, soy beans and corn
and stir to combine.
4 Working one at a time, dip a
tortilla into the sauce to coat both
sides, then put about 1/3 cup of the
filling across the centre and roll up to
enclose—it is easier if you do this in

the prepared dish. Place the
enchilada, seam-side-down, at one
end of the dish. Repeat with the
remaining filling and tortillas, lining
them up close together in the dish.
5 Pour the remaining sauce over
the enchiladas and sprinkle with the
cheese. Bake for 20–25 minutes, or
until the cheese has melted. Sprinkle
with chopped fresh parsley and serve
immediately, with a green salad.

NUTRITION PER SERVE
Protein 20 g; Fat 20 g; Carbohydrate 33 g;
Dietary Fibre 12 g; Cholesterol 0 mg;
1699 kJ (406 cal)

Combine the tomato mixture, pumpkin, soy beans and corn.

Dip one tortilla at a time into the tomato sauce.

Arrange the enchiladas seam-side-down in the dish.

CREAMY MUSHROOM AND LEEK SOY PASTA

Preparation time: 15 minutes
Total cooking time: 25 minutes
Serves 4–6

2 leeks
1 tablespoon soy spread or margarine
2 tablespoons soy bean oil
250 g button mushrooms
375 g soy pasta
150 g silken tofu, drained
2 tablespoons grated fresh Parmesan
100 ml cream
1 teaspoon fresh thyme, chopped
grated fresh Parmesan, extra,
    to serve
fresh thyme sprigs, to garnish

1 Wash the leeks thoroughly. Cut each in half lengthways and thinly slice. Heat the soy spread and 1 tablespoon of the oil in a large saucepan. Add the leek and cook over low heat for 10–12 minutes, or until soft—do not brown. Add the remaining oil, then the mushrooms. Cook for 7–10 minutes, or until soft. Remove from the heat and cover to keep warm.
2 Meanwhile, cook the pasta in a large saucepan of boiling water until *al dente*. Drain and keep warm.
3 Combine the tofu, Parmesan, cream and thyme in a food processor until smooth. Season with salt and freshly ground black pepper.

4 Return the leek and mushroom mixture to the heat and add the tofu cream mixture. Gently cook for 2–3 minutes, or until warmed through. Spoon the sauce over the pasta and garnish with the extra Parmesan and thyme sprigs.

NUTRITION PER SERVE (6)
Protein 12 g; Fat 20 g; Carbohydrate 39 g;
Dietary Fibre 9 g; Cholesterol 26 mg;
1629 kJ (389 cal)

Gently cook the sliced leek in the oil and soy spread until soft.

Blend the tofu, cream, Parmesan and thyme until smooth.

ORANGE SWEET POTATO AND TOFU GNOCCHI WITH ROASTED EGGPLANT

Preparation time: 45 minutes
Total cooking time: 50 minutes
Serves 4

500 g eggplant, cut into 2 cm cubes
1 tablespoon olive oil
1 large clove garlic, crushed
750 g orange sweet potato, peeled and cut into 3 cm chunks
250 g firm tofu
1 cup (125 g) plain flour
1 egg yolk
50 g soy spread
1 tablespoon fresh thyme leaves
2 tablespoons chopped fresh parsley
shaved Parmesan, extra, to garnish
fresh thyme sprigs, to garnish

1 Preheat the oven to moderately hot 200°C (400°F/Gas 6). Place the eggplant, oil and garlic in a bowl and toss together until well coated. Transfer to a baking tray. Bake for 20 minutes, or until browned and cooked through.
2 Meanwhile, steam the orange sweet potato for 10 minutes, or until tender. Drain and pat dry. Transfer to a bowl and mash with a potato masher. Drain the tofu well and gently pat dry with a clean cloth. Add to the orange sweet potato and mash together well. Add the flour and egg yolk and stir through. Season to taste with salt and freshly ground black pepper.
3 Turn the dough out onto a lightly floured surface, adding more flour if the mixture is too sticky—do not overwork or it will become gluey.

Bring the dough together into a ball with your hands.
4 Divide the dough into four portions and roll each portion on a lightly floured surface, to form a sausage shape about 2 cm in diameter. Cut into 2.5 cm pieces and shape each piece into an oval. Press each oval against a floured fork. As you make the gnocchi place them in a single layer on a baking tray, and cover until ready to cook.
5 Melt the soy spread in a small saucepan over medium heat. Add the thyme and cook, stirring, over low heat for 2 minutes.
6 Bring a large saucepan of salted water to the boil and cook the gnocchi in batches, for 3–4 minutes, or until the gnocchi rise to the surface. Remove with a slotted spoon and keep warm.
7 Add the eggplant and the parsley to the thyme mixture, return the pan to the heat and warm through for 2–3 minutes over medium heat. Season with salt and freshly ground black pepper. Divide the gnocchi among the serving bowls, top with the eggplant mixture and garnish with the Parmesan shavings and thyme sprigs.

NUTRITION PER SERVE
Protein 18 g; Fat 25 g; Carbohydrate 53 g; Dietary Fibre 7.5 g; Cholesterol 54 mg; 2123 kJ (507 cal)

COOK'S FILE
Note: Gnocchi are a small Italian dumpling related to pasta. Traditionally they are made from either pasta dough or from a mixture of potato flour and wheat flour, semolina or polenta.

Bake the eggplant in a moderately hot oven until browned and cooked through.

Stir in the flour, egg yolk, salt and pepper with a wooden spoon.

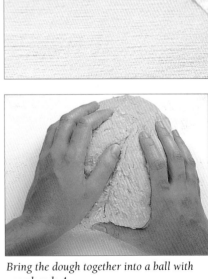

Bring the dough together into a ball with your hands.A

Roll each portion of dough into sausage-like lengths.

Form each 2.5 cm piece into an oval, then press gently with a fork.

Cook the gnocchi until they float to the surface. Remove with a slotted spoon.

MACARONI CHEESE

Preparation time: 10 minutes
Total cooking time: 30 minutes
Serves 4

500 g soy pasta twists
50 g soy spread
6 spring onions, finely sliced
1 tablespoon soy flour
1 litre soy milk
2 tablespoons cornflour dissolved
    in 2–3 tablespoons water
1 bay leaf
2¹/2 cups (310 g) grated vintage
    Cheddar
1 teaspoon paprika
1 tablespoon finely chopped fresh
    parsley

1 Preheat the oven to moderately hot 200°C (400°F/Gas 6). Cook the soy pasta in a large saucepan of boiling water until *al dente*. Drain, and transfer to a large bowl.
2 Melt the soy spread in a saucepan over medium heat. Add the spring onion and cook for 1–2 minutes, or until soft. Add the soy flour and cook, stirring, for 2 minutes. Remove the pan from the heat and whisk in the soy milk and cornflour mixture until the sauce is smooth.
3 Return to the heat, add the bay leaf and bring to the boil, stirring constantly. Reduce the heat and simmer, stirring, for 3 minutes. Remove the bay leaf and stir in 2 cups (250 g) of the cheese. Season well with salt and freshly ground black pepper. Pour the sauce over the pasta and mix together until well coated.
4 Spoon into a 3 litre ovenproof baking dish and sprinkle with the remaining cheese. Bake for 15 minutes, or until golden brown. Sprinkle with the paprika and parsley and serve immediately.

NUTRITION PER SERVE
Protein 37 g; Fat 42 g; Carbohydrate 83 g; Dietary Fibre 17 g; Cholesterol 76 mg; 3583 kJ (856 cal)

Add the soy flour to the spring onion and cook for 2 minutes.

Stir the sauce constantly until it thickens and is smooth.

BLACK BEAN AND CORIANDER PANCAKES WITH BOK CHOY

Preparation time: 30 minutes +
    10 minutes soaking
Total cooking time: 20 minutes
Serves 4

250 g baby bok choy, cut into
    quarters
1/2 cup (60 g) fermented black beans
3/4 cup (90 g) plain flour
3/4 cup (80 g) soy flour
1 teaspoon baking powder
4 eggs, lightly beaten
3/4 cup (185 ml) soy milk
1 cup (60 g) bean sprouts or soy bean
    sprouts
4 spring onions, thinly sliced
1/2 cup (15 g) fresh coriander leaves,
    finely chopped
1 tablespoon finely chopped fresh
    ginger
3 cloves garlic, finely chopped
2 small fresh red chillies, finely
    chopped
1 tablespoon sherry
3 tablespoons soy bean oil
1 clove garlic, crushed
sweet chilli sauce, to serve

1 Bring a large saucepan of salted water to the boil. Add the bok choy and cook for 2 minutes. Drain well and plunge into ice-cold water. Soak the black beans in water for 10 minutes. Drain.

2 Sift the flours and baking powder into a bowl and make a well in the centre. Combine the egg and milk, then whisk into the flour mixture until it forms a smooth paste. Add the black beans, sprouts, spring onion, coriander, ginger, garlic, chilli and sherry and mix well.

3 Heat 2 teaspoons soy bean oil in a large frying pan, wiping the surface lightly with paper towels to remove any excess oil. When hot, add 1/3 cup (80 ml) of the batter, spreading out to form a 10 cm wide pancake—depending on the size of your pan, you should be able to cook two at a time. Cook over medium heat for 1–2 minutes, or until small bubbles appear on the surface and the underneath is golden. Turn and cook for a further minute. Remove and keep warm. Repeat with the remaining batter to make 8 pancakes—add an extra 2 teaspoons oil, if necessary.

4 Heat the remaining soy bean oil in a frying pan or wok. Add the bok choy and stir-fry over medium heat for 2 minutes. Add the crushed garlic and cook for a further minute. Season well with salt and freshly ground black pepper. Arrange 2 pancakes on a serving plate, top with the bok choy and dollop with sweet chilli sauce on the side.

NUTRITION PER SERVE
Protein 20 g; Fat 26 g; Carbohydrate 26 g;
Dietary Fibre 7 g; Cholesterol 180 mg;
1724 kJ (412 cal)

Using tongs, plunge the blanched bok choy into ice-cold water.

Whisk the milk mixture into the dry ingredients to form a smooth paste.

Fry the pancakes until small bubbles appear on the surface.

MEATY MAIN MEALS

TERIYAKI BEEF AND SOY BEAN STIR-FRY

Preparation time: 15 minutes
Total cooking time: 20 minutes
Serves 4

400 g frozen soy beans
1 tablespoon peanut oil
700 g centre cut rump steak,
    cut into 1 cm x 5 cm strips
6 spring onions, finely sliced
2 cloves garlic, chopped
2 teaspoons finely chopped fresh
    ginger
50 g soy bean sprouts
1 red capsicum, finely sliced
1 tablespoon mirin
2 tablespoons sake
2 tablespoons Japanese soy sauce
2 teaspoons sugar

1 Place the soy beans in a saucepan of boiling water and cook for 2 minutes. Drain.
2 Heat a large wok until very hot. Add 2 teaspoons of the peanut oil and swirl to coat the side. Cook the beef in 3 batches for 3–4 minutes per batch, or until well browned. Remove from the wok and keep warm. Add the spring onion and stir-fry for 30 seconds, or until wilted.
3 Return the beef to the wok, add the garlic, ginger, soy beans, soy bean sprouts and capsicum, and stir-fry for 2 minutes. Combine the mirin, sake, Japanese soy sauce and sugar. Add the sauce to the wok and stir-fry until heated through. Serve hot with steamed rice.

NUTRITION PER SERVE
Protein 53 g; Fat 16 g; Carbohydrate 6.5 g; Dietary Fibre 6.5 g; Cholesterol 117 mg; 1590 kJ (380 cal)

COOK'S FILE
Notes: Frozen soy beans are available in packets, either in their pods or shelled. They are available from Asian food stores. This recipe uses the shelled variety.
Traditionally, teriyaki refers to kebabs that have been marinated, grilled and basted with teriyaki sauce (mirin, sake, soy sauce and sugar). Alternatively, such as the above dish, the meat can be stir-fried, then simmered in teriyaki sauce until it reduces to a glaze.
Variation: Chicken may be used instead of beef as a tasty alternative.

Cut the rump steak into strips using a sharp knife.

Toss the garlic, ginger, soy beans, sprouts, capsicum and meat.

BOSTON BAKED SOY BEANS

Preparation time: 15 minutes +
  overnight soaking
Total cooking time:
  5 hours 40 minutes
Serves 4–6

500 g dried soy beans
2 onions, chopped
1 tablespoon treacle
¼ cup (55 g) demerara sugar
3 teaspoons dried mustard
2 smoked pork hocks
  (about 600 g each)
2 tablespoons tomato sauce

1 Soak the soy beans in a large bowl of cold water for at least 8 hours, or preferably overnight. Drain. Place in a large saucepan and cover with fresh water. Bring to the boil and simmer for 2 hours—top up with water, if necessary. Drain and reserve 2 cups (500 ml) of the cooking liquid.

2 Preheat the oven to warm 160°C (315°F/Gas 2–3). Place the reserved cooking liquid in a 3.5 litre heavy-based casserole dish. Add the onion, treacle, demerara sugar, mustard and ½ teaspoon black pepper. Bring slowly to the boil. Reduce the heat and simmer for 2 minutes.

3 Add the beans and pork hocks. Bake, covered, for 3 hours, stirring once or twice during cooking—add a little water, if necessary, to keep the beans covered with liquid. Stir in the tomato sauce and bake, uncovered, for a further 30 minutes.

4 Remove the meat and skim any fat off the surface of the beans. Roughly shred the meat and return to the bean mixture. Serve hot.

NUTRITION PER SERVE (6)
Protein 55 g; Fat 19 g; Carbohydrate 23 g; Dietary Fibre 20 g; Cholesterol 60 mg; 2018 kJ (482 cal)

Bake the soy beans and pork hocks for 3 hours, topping up with water.

Remove the flesh from the bones and roughly shred.

CHINESE-STYLE STEAMED FISH

Preparation time: 15 minutes +
4 hours marinating
Total cooking time: 25 minutes
Serves 4

3 tablespoons white miso paste
1 tablespoon soy bean oil
2 cloves garlic, crushed
1 1/2 tablespoons grated fresh
ginger
2 tablespoons light soy sauce
2 tablespoons oyster sauce

1 large whole red snapper, cleaned and
scaled (about 1.5 kg)
4 spring onions, sliced on the
diagonal
fresh coriander leaves, to garnish

1 Combine the miso, oil, garlic, ginger, soy and oyster sauces in a food processor until smooth. Line a large bamboo steamer with baking paper—this makes it easier to remove the fish. If the fish is too big, cut off the head.
2 Make four deep diagonal slashes across both sides of the fish. Spoon half the paste over one side of the fish and rub well into the skin and slashes. Repeat on the other side

with the remaining paste. Place on a plate, cover with plastic wrap and refrigerate for 2–4 hours.
3 Place the fish in the steamer, top with the spring onion and steam over a wok of boiling water for 20–25 minutes, or until the fish is cooked through.
4 Remove the fish from the steamer, pour any juices collected in the baking paper over the top and garnish with coriander. Serve with steamed rice and stir-fried vegetables.

NUTRITION PER SERVE
Protein 77 g; Fat 12 g; Carbohydrate 4.5 g;
Dietary Fibre 1 g; Cholesterol 230 mg;
1840 kJ (440 cal)

Blend the miso, oil, garlic, ginger, soy and oyster sauces until smooth.

Cut deep diagonal slashes on both sides of the fish with a sharp knife.

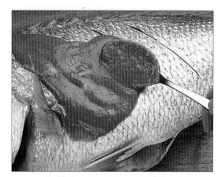

Spoon half the paste on top of the fish, rubbing well into the skin and slashes.

MISO YAKITORI CHICKEN

Preparation time: 30 minutes
Total cooking time: 20 minutes
Serves 4

3 tablespoons yellow or red miso
   paste
2 tablespoons sugar
¼ cup (60 ml) sake
2 tablespoons mirin
1 kg chicken thighs, boned (skin on)
1 cucumber
2 spring onions, cut into 2 cm pieces

1 Soak 12 long wooden bamboo skewers in cold water for at least 10 minutes. Place the miso, sugar, sake and mirin in a small saucepan over medium heat and cook, stirring well, for 2 minutes, or until the sauce is smooth and the sugar has dissolved completely.
2 Cut the chicken into 2.5 cm cubes. Seed the cucumber and cut into 2 cm batons. Thread the chicken, cucumber and spring onion alternately onto the skewers—you should have 3 pieces of chicken, 3 pieces of cucumber and 3 pieces of spring onion per skewer.

3 Cook on a grill plate over high heat, turning occasionally, for 10 minutes, or until the chicken is almost cooked. Brush with the miso sauce and continue cooking, then turn and brush the other side. Repeat this process once or twice until the chicken and vegetables are cooked. Serve immediately with steamed rice and salad.

NUTRITION PER SERVE
Protein 58 g; Fat 6.5 g; Carbohydrate 9 g;
Dietary Fibre 0.5 g; Cholesterol 126 mg;
1377 kJ (329 cal)

Remove the bones from the chicken thighs with a sharp knife.

Remove the seeds from the centre of the cucumber, then cut into batons.

Brush the chicken and vegetables with the miso sauce during cooking.

THAI-STYLE SEAFOOD CURRY WITH TOFU

Preparation time: 30 minutes
Total cooking time: 30 minutes
Serves 4

2 tablespoons soy bean oil
500 g firm white fish (ling, perch), cut into 2 cm cubes
250 g raw prawns, peeled and deveined, tails intact
2 x 400 ml cans coconut milk
1 tablespoon Thai red curry paste
4 fresh or 8 dried kaffir lime leaves
2 tablespoons fish sauce
2 tablespoons finely chopped fresh lemon grass (white part only)
2 cloves garlic, crushed
1 tablespoon finely chopped fresh galangal
1 tablespoon shaved palm sugar
300 g silken firm tofu, cut into 1.5 cm cubes
1/2 cup (60 g) bamboo shoots, julienned
1 large fresh red chilli, finely sliced
2 teaspoons lime juice
spring onions, chopped, to garnish
fresh coriander leaves, chopped, to garnish

1 Heat the oil in a large frying pan or wok. Sear the fish and prawns over medium heat for 1 minute on each side. Remove from the pan.
2 Place 1/4 cup (60 ml) coconut milk and the curry paste in the pan and cook over medium heat for 2 minutes, or until fragrant and the oil separates. Add the remaining coconut milk, kaffir lime leaves, fish sauce, lemon grass, garlic, galangal, palm sugar and 1 teaspoon salt. Cook over low heat for 15 minutes.
3 Add the tofu, bamboo shoots and chilli. Simmer for a further 3–5 minutes. Return to medium heat, add the seafood and lime juice and cook for a further 3 minutes, or until the seafood is just cooked. Remove from the heat.

4 Serve with steamed rice and garnish with the spring onion and coriander leaves.

NUTRITION PER SERVE
Protein 50 g; Fat 58 g; Carbohydrate 15 g; Dietary Fibre 4 g; Cholesterol 180 mg; 3201 kJ (765 cal)

Peel the prawns, remove the vein and keep the tails intact.

Cook the coconut milk and the curry paste until the oil separates.

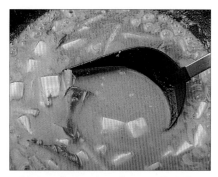
Add the tofu, bamboo shoots and chilli, then simmer for 5 minutes.

PROSCIUTTO AND VEGETABLE PASTA BAKE

Preparation time: 25 minutes
Total cooking time: 1 hour
Serves 6–8

3 tablespoons olive oil
1/3 cup (35 g) dried breadcrumbs
250 g soy pasta
6 thin slices prosciutto, chopped
1 red onion, chopped
1 red capsicum, chopped
1/2 cup (100 g) semi-dried tomatoes,
   roughly chopped
3 tablespoons shredded fresh basil
1 cup (100 g) grated fresh Parmesan
4 eggs, lightly beaten
1 cup (250 ml) soy milk

1 Preheat the oven to moderate 180°C (350°F/Gas 4). Grease a 25 cm round ovenproof ceramic dish with a little of the olive oil and sprinkle the dish with 2 tablespoons of the breadcrumbs to coat the base and side. Cook the pasta in a large saucepan of boiling water until *al dente*. Drain and transfer to a large bowl.
2 Heat 1 tablespoon of the remaining oil in a large frying pan. Add the prosciutto and onion and cook over medium heat for 4–5 minutes, or until softened and golden in colour. Add the capsicum and semi-dried tomato and cook for a further 1–2 minutes. Add to the pasta with the basil and Parmesan and toss together well. Spoon the mixture into the prepared dish.
3 Place the eggs and milk in a bowl, whisk together, then season to taste with salt and freshly ground black pepper. Pour the egg mixture over the pasta. Season the remaining breadcrumbs with salt and freshly ground black pepper, add the remaining oil and toss together. Sprinkle the seasoned breadcrumb mixture over the pasta. Bake for 40 minutes, or until set. Allow to stand for 5 minutes, then cut into wedges and serve with a green salad, if desired.

NUTRITION PER SERVE (8)
Protein 14 g; Fat 13 g; Carbohydrate 25 g; Dietary Fibre 5 g; Cholesterol 100 mg; 1126 kJ (270 cal)

Drain the cooked pasta, then transfer to a large bowl.

Cook the prosciutto, onion, capsicum and semi-dried tomato.

Pour the egg and milk mixture over the pasta and vegetables.

CHILLI CON CARNE WITH SOY BEANS

Preparation time: 15 minutes
Total cooking time:
    1 hour 25 minutes
Serves 4

1 tablespoon soy bean oil
2 onions, chopped
2 cloves garlic, crushed
650 g beef mince
1 teaspoon paprika
1/2 teaspoon ground cumin
1 1/2 teaspoons chilli powder
415 g can chopped tomatoes
2 tablespoons tomato paste
2 tablespoons polenta
1 1/2 cups (375 ml) beef stock
420 g can soy beans, rinsed and
    drained
1/3 cup (20 g) chopped fresh parsley

1 Heat the oil in a heavy-based
2.5 litre flameproof casserole dish.
Add the onion and garlic and cook
over medium heat for 5 minutes, or
until softened. Increase the heat to
high and add the mince. Cook,
stirring, for 3–4 minutes, or until the
mince changes colour, breaking up
any lumps with a wooden spoon.
2 Reduce the heat to medium, add
the paprika, ground cumin, chilli
powder, 1/2 teaspoon salt and
1/2 teaspoon freshly ground black
pepper. Cook, stirring, for a further
1 minute. Stir in the chopped tomato,
tomato paste, polenta and stock
and bring to the boil. Reduce the
heat and simmer, partially covered,
for 1 hour. Stir in the soy beans
and cook, covered, for a further
10 minutes. Garnish with the
chopped parsley and serve with
rice and corn chips.

NUTRITION PER SERVE
Protein 44 g; Fat 29 g; Carbohydrate 13 g;
Dietary Fibre 8 g; Cholesterol 100 mg;
2040 kJ (488 cal)

Stir the mixture until the mince changes colour, breaking up any lumps.

Stir in the tomato, tomato paste and polenta, then pour in the stock.

VEGETABLE AND PRAWN TEMPURA

Preparation time: 45 minutes
Total cooking time: 20 minutes
Serves 4

8 cap mushrooms
1 green capsicum
1 sheet dried nori
12 green beans, cut in half
300 g silken firm tofu, cut into
    2 cm cubes
1 small (400 g) eggplant
8 large raw prawns, peeled and
    deveined, tails intact
vegetable oil, for deep-frying
2/3 cup (80 g) soy flour
1 1/3 cup (165 g) plain flour
475 ml chilled soda water
2 egg yolks, lightly beaten
3 tablespoons plain flour, extra,
    for dusting
100 g daikon radish, peeled and
    finely shredded
2 tablespoons grated fresh ginger

Dipping sauce
300 ml dashi
1/3 cup (80 ml) soy sauce
1/3 cup (80 ml) mirin

1   Wipe the mushroom caps clean and trim the stalks. Cut the capsicum into strips, then trim the end off the strips to form flat even-sized batons. Cut a narrow strip of nori and tie the beans together in groups of three, wetting the end of the nori to seal it. Pat the tofu dry with paper towels. Thinly slice the eggplant lengthways, then in half crossways. Place the prepared vegetables and prawns on a tray.

2   Fill a deep heavy-based saucepan one third full of oil and heat to 170°C (325°F), or until a cube of bread browns in 20 seconds.
3   Place the soy and plain flours in a large bowl and make a well in the centre. Pour in the soda water and egg yolk and loosely mix together with chopsticks or a fork until just combined—the batter should be quite thick and lumpy.
4   Coat the prawns and vegetables in the extra plain flour. Dip in the batter then deep-fry in batches, turning occasionally, for 1–3 minutes, or until crisp and golden and cooked

through—do not overcrowd the pan. Remove with a slotted spoon and drain on paper towels. Between batches, skim off the bits of batter floating in the oil.
5   To make the dipping sauce, combine the dashi, soy sauce and mirin in a small saucepan. Bring to the boil then turn off the heat. Serve with the vegetable and prawn tempura and small mounds of shredded daikon and ginger.

NUTRITION PER SERVE
Protein 33 g; Fat 20 g; Carbohydrate 56 g; Dietary Fibre 8.5 g; Cholesterol 145 mg; 2302 kJ (550 cal)

Secure the beans with a strip of nori and dampen the end with water to seal.

Lightly mix the soda water and egg into the flours with chopsticks.

Using chopsticks, dip the prawns and the prepared vegetables into the batter.

TOMATO, BACON AND SOY BEAN SOUP WITH POLENTA STICKS

Preparation time: 20 minutes +
   overnight soaking +
   1 hour chilling
Total cooking time:
   3 hours 10 minutes
Serves 4

1/2 cup (120 g) dried soy beans
1 1/2 tablespoons soy bean oil
1 onion, finely chopped
4 rashers bacon, diced
800 g tomatoes, peeled and
   chopped (if using canned
   tomatoes, do not drain)
1 sprig basil, whole
3 cups (750 ml) chicken stock
fresh basil, extra, chopped, to garnish

Polenta sticks
1 1/2 cups (375 ml) soy milk
1/2 cup (75 g) polenta
1/4 cup (25 g) freshly grated Parmesan
1 teaspoon finely chopped fresh
   rosemary
30 g soy spread
1/4 cup (30 g) plain flour
soy oil, for deep-frying

1 Soak the soy beans in a large bowl with plenty of cold water for at least 8 hours or overnight. Rinse well. Transfer to a saucepan, cover with cold water and simmer for 2 hours, or until tender. Drain.
2 Heat the oil in a saucepan. Add the onion and bacon and cook for 5 minutes, or until soft. Add the tomato and cook for 5 minutes, or until pulpy. Stir in the basil, stock and 1 cup (250 ml) water. Bring to

the boil, reduce the heat and simmer for 20 minutes. Add the beans and heat through.
3 To make the polenta sticks, place the soy milk and 1 1/2 cups (375 ml) water in a saucepan. Bring to the boil over high heat and add 1/2 teaspoon salt. Reduce to low and add the polenta in a steady stream, whisking constantly to prevent lumps. Simmer, stirring with a wooden spoon, for 20–25 minutes, or until it pulls away from the side of the pan. Add the Parmesan, rosemary and soy spread and mix well. Season to taste.
4 Grease a 12 x 22 cm loaf tin. Spoon the polenta into the tin and smooth the surface with a wet spatula. Chill in the refrigerator for at least 1 hour (preferably overnight), or until set. Cut the polenta into

24 sticks (1.5 x 9 cm) and lightly coat in plain flour.
5 Fill a heavy-based saucepan one third full with the soy oil and heat to 170°C (325°F), or until a cube of bread browns in 20 seconds. Deep-fry in batches for 2 minutes, or until golden brown all over—turn with tongs. Drain well.
6 Spoon the soup into bowls and season to taste. Garnish with extra basil and serve with polenta sticks.

NUTRITION PER SERVE
Protein 27 g; Fat 39 g; Carbohydrate 30 g; Dietary Fibre 9.5 g; Cholesterol 25 mg; 2313 kJ (553 cal)

COOK'S FILE
Note: To reheat leftover polenta sticks, place on a baking tray and heat at 180°C (350°F/Gas 4) for 6 minutes.

Add the tomato to the bacon mixture and cook until pulpy.

Spoon the polenta into the loaf tin and smooth the surface with a spatula.

Deep-fry the polenta sticks until golden brown all over.

CHINESE BEEF IN SOY

Preparation time: 20 minutes +
  overnight marinating
Total cooking time:
  1 hour 45 minutes
Serves 4

700 g chuck steak, trimmed and
  cut into 2 cm cubes
1/3 cup (80 ml) dark soy sauce
2 tablespoons honey
1 tablespoon wine vinegar
3 tablespoons soy bean oil
4 cloves garlic, chopped
8 spring onions, finely sliced
1 tablespoon finely grated fresh ginger

2 star anise
1/2 teaspoon ground cloves
1 1/2 cups (375 ml) beef stock
1/2 cup (125 ml) red wine
spring onions, extra, sliced, to garnish

1 Place the meat in a non-metallic
dish. Combine the soy sauce, honey
and vinegar in a small bowl, then
pour over the meat. Cover with
plastic wrap and marinate for at least
2 hours, or preferably overnight.
Drain, reserving the marinade, and
pat the cubes dry.
2 Place 1 tablespoon of the oil in a
saucepan and brown the meat in
3 batches, for 3–4 minutes per
batch—add another tablespoon of
oil, if necessary. Remove the meat.

Add the remaining oil and fry the
garlic, spring onion, ginger, star anise
and cloves for 1–2 minutes, or until
fragrant.
3 Return all the meat to the pan,
add the reserved marinade, stock and
wine. Bring to the boil and simmer,
covered, for 1 hour 15 minutes.
Cook, uncovered, for a further
15 minutes, or until the sauce is
syrupy and the meat is tender.
4 Garnish with the extra sliced
spring onions and serve immediately
with steamed rice.

NUTRITION PER SERVE
Protein 37 g; Fat 20 g; Carbohydrate 12 g;
Dietary Fibre 0.5 g; Cholesterol 117 mg;
1657 kJ (395 cal)

*Finely grate a piece of fresh ginger on a
wooden ginger grater.*

*Cook the cubes of beef, in batches, until
brown all over.*

**Simmer the beef, marinade, stock and
wine until the sauce is thick and syrupy.**

SPICY NOODLES WITH PORK AND TOFU

Preparation time: 20 minutes
Total cooking time: 15 minutes
Seves 4

250 g Hokkien noodles
1 tablespoon oil
500 g pork fillet, thinly sliced
2 cloves garlic, crushed
2 cm x 2 cm piece fresh ginger,
    julienned
100 g snow peas, sliced
100 g fresh shiitake mushrooms, sliced

1/2 teaspoon five-spice powder
2 tablespoons hoisin sauce
2 tablespoons soy sauce
1/4 cup (60 ml) vegetable stock
200 g fried tofu, sliced
100 g soy bean sprouts
fried red Asian shallot flakes,
    to garnish

1 Cook the noodles in a large saucepan of boiling water for 2–3 minutes, or until tender. Drain.
2 Heat a wok over high heat, add half the oil and swirl to coat. Add the pork in two batches and stir-fry for 2 minutes each batch, or until browned. Remove from the wok.

3 Add a little more oil if necessary, then add the garlic and ginger and stir-fry for 30 seconds, or until fragrant. Add the snow peas, mushrooms and five-spice powder and cook for a further 1 minute. Pour in the hoisin sauce, soy sauce and stock and cook, stirring constantly, for 1–2 minutes. Add the tofu, soy bean sprouts, noodles and pork and toss to warm through.
4 Serve immediately, garnished with the fried shallot flakes.

NUTRITION PER SERVE
Protein 45 g; Fat 16 g; Carbohydrate 55 g; Dietary Fibre 9.5 g; Cholesterol 75 mg; 2293 kJ (548 cal)

Use a sharp knife to slice the pork fillets into thin slices.

Stir-fry the pork slices in batches until browned all over.

Add the hoisin and soy sauces and stock and cook for a further 1–2 minutes.

ROAST DINNER
(SERVES SIX)

FIVE-SPICE SOY CHICKEN

Combine *1/4 cup (60 ml) Japanese soy sauce, 1/4 cup (60 ml) Chinese rice wine, 2 cloves crushed garlic, 1 tablespoon finely chopped fresh ginger, 1/4 cup (90 g) honey, 1/2 teaspoon five-spice powder, 2 tablespoons soy bean oil* and *2 teaspoons hot bean sauce* in a large ceramic dish. Add a *2 kg chicken* and turn to coat. Spoon some marinade into the cavity. Cover and refrigerate overnight. Preheat the oven to moderately hot 200°C (400°F/Gas 6). Drain and reserve the marinade. Place the chicken on a rack in a roasting tin and pour *2 cups (500 ml) water* in the base of the tin. Roast for 1 hour, basting regularly with the reserved marinade (cover with foil if it overbrowns). Maintain the water level in the base of the tin. Cover loosely with foil and rest for 15 minutes before carving. To make the gravy, melt *1 tablespoon soy spread* in a small saucepan, stir in *3 tablespoons soy flour* and cook for 1 minute. Whisk in the roasting tin juices and the reserved marinade and simmer for 10 minutes, or until smooth and thickened slightly.

PUMPKIN WITH MISO GLAZE

Peel and seed *1 butternut pumpkin (600 g)* and cut into 6 flat even pieces. Boil for 12 minutes, or until tender. Drain and cool. Preheat the oven to hot 220°C (425°F/Gas 7) and place the pumpkin on a greased baking tray. Combine *2 tablespoons white miso, 1 tablespoon mirin, 1 tablespoon sake, 1 tablespoon lemon juice* and *1 teaspoon soft brown sugar*. Spread evenly on one flat side of the pumpkin then sprinkle with *2 teaspoons sesame seeds*. Bake for 15 minutes, or until the pumpkin is cooked through. Garnish with *finely sliced spring onion*.

CAULIFLOWER CHEESE

Boil *500 g cauliflower florets* for 6 minutes, or until tender. Drain. Preheat the oven to moderately hot 200°C (400°F/Gas 6). Melt *2 tablespoons soy spread* in a saucepan, stir in *4 tablespoons soy flour* and cook over medium heat for 1 minute. Take off the heat and whisk in *11/2 cups (375 ml) soy milk*. Return to the heat and simmer, stirring, for 5 minutes, or until slightly thickened. Stir in *200 g grated soy cheese* and *1/2 cup (50 g) grated fresh Parmesan* until melted, then add *2 teaspoons Dijon mustard, 2 finely chopped spring onions* and a *pinch of cayenne pepper*. Season. Place the florets in a greased 1.5 litre rectangular ovenproof dish. Pour on the cheese sauce and sprinkle *1/3 cup (40 g) grated soy cheese* combined with *1/4 cup (25 g) grated fresh Parmesan*. Bake for 25 minutes, or until golden.

POTATO AND CORIANDER MASH

Boil *750 g chopped desiree potatoes* with *4 cloves garlic* for 20 minutes, or until tender. Drain. Return to the pan with *250 g drained crumbled silken tofu, 2 tablespoons soy spread* and *1/3 cup (90 g) soy mayonnaise*—mash until smooth and creamy. Stir in *1/4 cup (25 g) finely chopped fresh coriander leaves*. Season with salt and pepper.

SOY BEANS WITH SPRING ONIONS AND SNOW PEAS

Trim *525 g bulb spring onions* leaving 1 cm of green. Peel off the outer layer and trim the root ends, leaving them intact. Boil for 1 minute. Drain and cool slightly. Halve each onion lengthways. Melt *1 tablespoon soy spread* in a small frying pan. Add the onions, cut-side-down and cook over medium heat for 3–4 minutes, or until well browned. Boil *400 g frozen soy beans* for 3 minutes, or until tender, adding *100 g snow peas* in the last minute. Drain. Toss with the onions, *1 tablespoon soy spread* and *1 teaspoon soy sauce*.

Clockwise from left: Five-spice soy chicken, Pumpkin with miso glaze, Cauliflower cheese, Potato and coriander mash, Soy beans with spring onions and snow peas.

TUNA STEAKS AND SOY BEAN SALAD

Preparation time: 35 minutes
Total cooking time: 10 minutes
Serves 4

Ginger dressing
¼ cup (60 ml) soy bean oil
2 tablespoons white wine vinegar
1 tablespoon grated fresh ginger
2 teaspoons honey
2 teaspoons salt-reduced soy sauce

2 carrots, sliced on the diagonal
2 zucchini, sliced on the diagonal
1 red capsicum, cut into 2 cm cubes
4 tuna steaks (about 180 g each),
    cubed
soy bean oil, for brushing
½ small red onion, cut into thin
    wedges
150 g cherry tomatoes, halved
300 g can soy beans, rinsed and
    drained
1 tablespoon baby capers
125 g baby rocket leaves

1 To make the ginger dressing, place the oil, vinegar, ginger, honey and soy sauce in a jar and shake well.
2 Bring a saucepan of water to the boil. Add the carrot, zucchini and capsicum and cook, covered, for 1 minute. Drain and cool quickly under cold running water. Drain well.
3 Pat the tuna cubes dry with paper towels, then brush lightly with a little oil. Cook on a hot chargrill or barbecue plate for 1–2 minutes each side, or until cooked to your liking—the centre should still be pink.
4 Place the blanched vegetables, onion, tomato, soy beans, capers and rocket in a large bowl. Add the dressing and toss together. Divide among four serving bowls and toss in the cubes of tuna. Serve immediately.

NUTRITION PER SERVE
Protein 35 g; Fat 30 g; Carbohydrate 10 g; Dietary Fibre 7 g; Cholesterol 50 mg; 1359 kJ (325 cal)

Rinse the canned beans with cold water and drain well.

Vigorously shake the ginger dressing ingredients in a jar to combine.

Chargrill the cubes of tuna until cooked to your liking.

Drain the soaked and cooked soy beans well in a colander.

Cook the sausages in a frying pan, turning frequently, until brown all over.

Simmer the tomato mixture until reduced and thickened slightly.

Return the casserole dish to the stove top and skim off any fat.

PORK SAUSAGE, SOY BEAN AND TOMATO CASSEROLE

Preparation time: 25 minutes + overnight soaking
Total cooking time: 4 hours
Serves 4

1½ cups (325 g) dried soy beans
8 thin pork sausages (575 g)
2 tablespoons soy bean oil
1 red onion, chopped
4 cloves garlic, chopped
1 large carrot, diced
1 celery stick, diced
2 x 415 g cans chopped tomatoes
1 tablespoon tomato paste
1 cup (250 ml) white wine
2 sprigs fresh thyme
1 teaspoon dried oregano leaves
1 tablespoon fresh oregano, chopped

1 Soak the soy beans in a large bowl of cold water for at least 8 hours, or overnight. Drain well. Place in a large saucepan with enough fresh water to cover. Bring to the boil, then reduce the heat and slowly simmer for 1 hour 15 minutes to 2 hours—keep the beans covered with water during cooking. Drain.

2 Prick the sausages all over. Heat a frying pan and cook, turning, for 10 minutes, or until browned all over. Drain on paper towels.

3 Heat the oil in a 3.5 litre flameproof casserole dish. Add the onion and garlic and cook on the stove top over medium heat for 3–5 minutes, or until softened. Add the carrot and celery. Cook, stirring, for a further 5 minutes. Stir in the tomato, paste, wine, thyme and dried oregano and bring to the boil. Reduce the heat and simmer, stirring often, for 10 minutes, or until the liquid has reduced and thickened slightly.

4 Preheat the oven to warm 160°C (315°F/Gas 2–3). Add the sausages, beans and 1 cup (250 ml) water to the casserole dish. Bake, covered, for 2 hours. Stir occasionally, adding more water if necessary to keep the beans just covered.

5 Return the casserole dish to the stove top, skim off any fat, then reduce the liquid until thickened slightly. Remove the thyme sprigs and stir through the fresh oregano.

NUTRITION PER SERVE
Protein 46 g; Fat 58 g; Carbohydrate 20 g; Dietary Fibre 23 g; Cholesterol 93 mg; 3479 kJ (830 cal)

PHAD THAI WITH TOFU, CHICKEN AND PRAWNS

Preparation time: 25 minutes +
  10 minutes soaking
Total cooking time: 10 minutes
Serves 4

250 g dried wide rice stick noodles
2 tablespoons soy bean oil
3 cloves garlic, finely chopped
2 small fresh red chillies, seeded
  and chopped
150 g chicken breast fillet, thinly
  sliced
200 g raw prawns, peeled and
  deveined, tails intact
100 g fried tofu, julienned (see Note)
3 tablespoons fish sauce
3 tablespoons lime juice
3 teaspoons palm or soft brown sugar
1 cup (90 g) soy bean sprouts,
  trimmed
¼ cup (45 g) unsalted roasted
  peanuts, chopped

3 tablespoons coriander leaves
lime wedges, to garnish

1 Soak the noodles in warm water
for 10 minutes, or until soft. Drain.
2 Heat a large wok or frying pan
until hot, add the oil and swirl to
coat. Add the garlic, chilli and
chicken and stir-fry for 2 minutes.
Stir in the prawns and cook for a
further 2 minutes. Toss through the
noodles and tofu until heated.
3 Add the fish sauce, lime juice and

sugar and gently toss until well
combined and heated through.
4 Spoon onto a platter and sprinkle
with the sprouts, peanuts and
coriander. Garnish with lime wedges.

NUTRITION PER SERVE
Protein 27 g; Fat 20 g; Carbohydrate 20 g;
Dietary Fibre 4 g; Cholesterol 90 mg;
1505 kJ (360 cal)

COOK'S FILE
Note: Fried tofu is a pre-cooked
product found in Asian food stores.

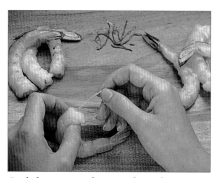

Peel the prawns, leaving the tails intact.
Slit the back and pull out the vein.

Briefly stir-fry the prawns with the
garlic, chilli and chicken.

SALMON WITH MISO AND SOY NOODLES

Preparation time: 20 minutes
Total cooking time: 15 minutes
Serves 6

300 g soba noodles
1 tablespoon soy bean oil
3 teaspoons white miso paste
100 ml honey
1½ tablespoons sesame oil
6 salmon fillets, boned and skin
   removed
1 teaspoon chopped garlic
1 tablespoon grated fresh ginger
1 carrot, julienned
6 small spring onions, thinly sliced
1 cup (70 g) soy bean sprouts
⅓ cup (80 ml) rice vinegar
3 tablespoons light soy sauce
1 teaspoon sesame oil, extra
1 tablespoon toasted sesame seeds
mustard cress, to garnish

1 Preheat the oven to moderate 180°C (350°F/Gas 4). Fill a large saucepan three quarters full with water and bring to the boil. Add the soba noodles and return to the boil. Cook for 1 minute, then add 1 cup (250 ml) cold water. Boil for 1–2 minutes, then add another 1 cup (250 ml) water. Boil for 2 minutes, or until tender, then drain and toss with ½ teaspoon of the soy bean oil.
2 Combine the miso, honey, sesame oil and 1 tablespoon water to form a paste. Brush over the salmon, then sear on a hot chargrill for 30 seconds on each side. Brush the salmon with the remaining paste and place on a baking tray. Bake for 6 minutes, then cover and rest in a warm place.

3 Heat the remaining soy oil in a wok. Add the garlic, ginger, carrot, spring onion and sprouts, and stir-fry for 1 minute—the vegetables should not brown, but remain crisp and bright. Add the noodles, rice vinegar, soy sauce and extra sesame oil and stir-fry quickly to heat through.
4 Divide the noodles among six

serving plates and top with a portion of salmon and sprinkle with the sesame seeds. Garnish with the mustard cress and serve.

NUTRITION PER SERVE
Protein 8 g; Fat 9.5 g; Carbohydrate 56 g; Dietary Fibre 2.5 g; Cholesterol 9 mg; 1423 kJ (340 cal)

Place the cooked soba noodles in a large bowl and toss with the soy oil.

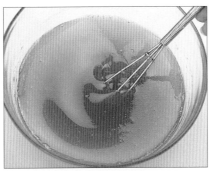

Whisk together the miso, honey, sesame oil and water.

Stir-fry the vegetables, without browning, until crisp and bright.

MA PO TOFU WITH BEEF MINCE

Preparation time: 15 minutes +
    5 minutes soaking
Total cooking time: 10 minutes
Serves 4–6

2 tablespoons fermented black beans
2 tablespoons vegetable oil
200 g minced beef
1 tablespoon finely chopped fresh
    ginger
3 spring onions, finely chopped
½ cup (125 ml) vegetable stock
2 tablespoons soy sauce
1 tablespoon chilli bean paste
2 tablespoons Chinese rice wine
450 g firm tofu, cut into 1.5 cm cubes
2 cloves garlic, coarsely chopped
1 tablespoon cornflour
2 teaspoons sesame oil

1 Place the black beans in a bowl of cold water and soak for 5 minutes. Drain and finely chop.
2 Heat the oil in a wok or non-stick frying pan. Add the mince and season with salt and freshly ground black pepper. Stir-fry over high heat for 2 minutes, or until the meat changes colour—use a wooden spoon to break up any lumps. Add the black beans, ginger and spring onion and stir-fry for a further 2 minutes.
3 Stir in the vegetable stock, soy sauce, chilli bean paste and rice wine. Add the tofu and garlic, and stir gently until the tofu is well coated with the sauce. Leave to cook over low heat for a further 3 minutes.
4 Combine the cornflour with 3 tablespoons water until it forms a smooth paste. Add the cornflour mixture and sesame oil to the wok. Stir over medium heat for 1 minute, or until thickened slightly. Serve immediately with boiled rice.

NUTRITION PER SERVE (6)
Protein 12 g; Fat 20 g; Carbohydrate 2.5 g;
Dietary Fibre 0 g; Cholesterol 20 mg;
1067 kJ (255 cal)

Cut the firm tofu into cubes with a sharp knife.

Soak and drain the fermented black beans, then finely chop.

Stir-fry the mince with the black beans, ginger and spring onion.

SOY BEAN MOUSSAKA

Preparation time: 30 minutes
Total cooking time:
   1 hour 20 minutes
Serves 4–6

500 g eggplant, cut into 1 cm slices
soy bean oil, for brushing
2 tablespoons soy bean oil, extra
1 large onion, chopped
2 cloves garlic, chopped
650 g minced lamb
2 tablespoons tomato paste
415 g can chopped tomatoes
1 cup (250 ml) white wine or water
1 teaspoon ground cinnamon
1/3 cup (20 g) chopped fresh parsley
1 teaspoon chopped fresh oregano
300 g can soy beans, rinsed and
   drained

Cheese sauce
75 g soy spread or margarine
1/3 cup (40 g) plain flour
2 1/2 cups (625 ml) soy milk
1/2 cup (60 g) grated Cheddar
1/2 teaspoon ground nutmeg
1 egg

1 Brush the eggplant slices with soy bean oil. Chargrill, or grill under a hot grill, for 2–3 minutes on each side, or until golden brown and softened. Keep warm.
2 Heat the extra soy bean oil in a frying pan. Add the onion and garlic and cook over medium heat for 5 minutes, or until softened. Increase the heat and add the mince. Cook, stirring, for 5 minutes, or until the mince changes colour—use a wooden spoon to break up any lumps.
3 Reduce the heat and add the tomato paste, tomatoes, wine, cinnamon, parsley and oregano. Simmer for 15 minutes, or until the liquid has been absorbed. Season well with salt and pepper, then stir in the beans. Preheat the oven to moderate 180°C (350°F/Gas 4).
4 To make the cheese sauce, heat the soy spread in a saucepan. Stir in the flour and cook, stirring, for 1 minute. Remove from the heat and whisk in the soy milk. Return to the heat and stir constantly until thickened. Cook for a further 2 minutes, then remove from the heat and stir in the cheese and nutmeg. Season well with salt and ground black pepper. Leave for 5 minutes then whisk in the egg.
5 Spoon one third of the meat and bean mixture on the base of a 1.5 litre casserole dish and arrange one third of the eggplant slices on top. Layer twice more ending with the eggplant slices, pressing down firmly and evenly with the back of a spoon. Pour on the sauce and bake for 50 minutes, or until the top is set and golden brown. Serve hot.

NUTRITION PER SERVE (6)
Protein 47 g; Fat 50 g; Carbohydrate 20 g; Dietary Fibre 14 g; Cholesterol 108 mg; 2992 kJ (715 cal)

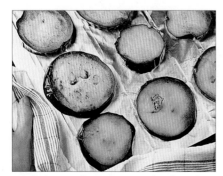

Grill the eggplant slices until softened and both sides are golden brown.

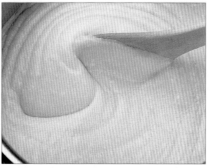

Stir the cheese sauce constantly with a wooden spoon until it thickens.

Pour the cheese sauce over the top layer of eggplant slices.

DESSERTS

BLUEBERRY CHEESECAKE

Preparation time: 20 minutes +
2 hours chilling
Total cooking time: 10 minutes
Serves 6–8

250 g wholemeal biscuits
3 teaspoons ground cinnamon
150 g soy spread or margarine,
    melted
1 1/2 tablespoons gelatine
250 g silken firm tofu
1/4 cup (60 g) caster sugar
250 g cream cheese
300 g vanilla soy yoghurt
300 g blueberries (see Note)

1 Preheat the oven to moderate 180°C (350°F/Gas 4). Grease a 23 cm springform tin.
2 Place the biscuits and 1 teaspoon of the ground cinnamon in a food processor and blend together until it forms fine crumbs. Transfer to a bowl, add the melted soy spread and mix well. Press the crumb mixture onto the base of the prepared tin. Bake for 10 minutes, then cool.
3 Pour 2/3 cup (170 ml) water into a heatproof bowl, evenly sprinkle on the gelatine and leave until spongy—do not stir. Bring a saucepan of water to the boil and remove from the heat. Place the bowl of gelatine in the pan and stir until the gelatine is smooth.

4 Combine the tofu, sugar, cream cheese and yoghurt in a food processor until smooth. Add the gelatine and process in short bursts for 1–2 seconds.
5 Place the blueberries on the biscuit base and pour the tofu mixture over the top, spreading evenly. Chill for at least 2 hours.
6 Remove the side of the tin and dust the cheesecake with the remaining ground cinnamon just before serving.

NUTRITION PER SERVE (8)
Protein 12 g; Fat 32 g; Carbohydrate 34 g; Dietary Fibre 4 g; Cholesterol 36 mg; 1978 kJ (470 cal)

COOK'S FILE
Note: Fresh blueberries are best for this recipe, but are not always available. If they are not in season, use 400 g canned well-drained blueberries or 300 g frozen blueberries, thawed.
Variation: Any other berries, such as raspberries, blackberries, boysenberries and strawberries (or even a combination of all or any of the above) can be used instead of the blueberries. Keep the gram measure of fruit(s) the same.
Storage: This cheesecake will keep for 4–5 days, stored in an airtight container in the refrigerator. It is not suitable to freeze.

Press the crumb mixture onto the base of the tin with the back of a spoon.

Gently pour the tofu and cream cheese mixture over the blueberries.

Melt the chocolate in a heatproof bowl over a saucepan of simmering water.

Beat the egg whites together until soft peaks form.

Gently fold the egg whites into the chocolate mixture.

CHOCOLATE MOUSSE

Preparation time: 25 minutes +
   3 hours chilling
Total cooking time: Nil
Serves 4

100 g good-quality dark
   chocolate
1 tablespoon brandy
200 g silken tofu
3 eggs, separated
1 tablespoon caster sugar
dark chocolate, extra, grated,
   to garnish

1 Roughly chop the chocolate and melt in a heatproof bowl over a saucepan of simmering water—do not let the base of the bowl touch the water. Remove the bowl from the heat and leave to cool slightly.
2 Combine the chocolate, brandy, tofu and egg yolks in a food processor. Transfer to a bowl.
3 Beat the egg whites until soft peaks form. Continue beating and gradually add the sugar. Thoroughly mix 1 tablespoon of the egg white mixture into the chocolate then gently fold the rest through until well combined.
4 Divide the mixture among four 150 ml ramekins or individual serving bowls and refrigerate for 2–3 hours, or until set. Serve with cream or soy yoghurt and garnish with grated chocolate.

NUTRITION PER SERVE
Protein 9.5 g; Fat 13 g; Carbohydrate 21 g;
Dietary Fibre 0 g; Cholesterol 135 mg;
1020 kJ (244 cal)

COOK'S FILE
Note: Brandy can be substituted with a different flavoured liqueur (such as coffee, almond or hazelnut). You can also try stirring through a couple of tablespoons of finely chopped toasted nuts before setting, for added texture and flavour.

CARAMEL RICE PUDDING

Preparation time: 15 minutes
Total cooking time:
    1 hour 15 minutes
Serves 4

1/2 cup (120 g) medium-grain or
    short-grain rice
2 eggs
2 tablespoons soft brown sugar
1 1/2 cups (375 ml) vanilla-flavoured
    soy milk

2 tablespoons caramel topping
1/2 cup (125 ml) cream
1/2 teaspoon ground nutmeg
ground nutmeg, extra, to garnish

1 Preheat the oven to warm 160°C (315°F/Gas 2–3). Grease a 1.5 litre ovenproof ceramic dish. Cook the rice in a saucepan of boiling water for 12 minutes, or until just tender. Drain and cool slightly.

2 Place the eggs, brown sugar, soy milk, caramel topping and cream in a large bowl and whisk together well. Fold in the rice. Pour the mixture into the prepared dish and sprinkle the surface with the nutmeg. Place the ceramic dish in a deep baking tin and pour in enough boiling water to come halfway up the sides.

3 Bake for 30 minutes, then stir with a fork to distribute the rice evenly. Cook for a further 30 minutes, or until the custard is just set. Serve hot or warm. Sprinkle with the extra ground nutmeg just before serving.

NUTRITION PER SERVE
Protein 8.5 g; Fat 20 g; Carbohydrate 42 g; Dietary Fibre 0.5 g; Cholesterol 133 mg; 1477 kJ (353 cal)

Gently fold the cooked rice into the caramel cream mixture.

Place the ceramic dish in a baking tin and fill halfway with boiling water.

Stir with a fork, halfway through cooking, to evenly distribute the rice.

FROZEN MANGO AND BANANA TERRINE

Preparation time: 20 minutes +
  overnight freezing
Total cooking time: Nil
Serves 6

soy bean oil, for greasing
1 cup (90 g) shredded coconut
125 g silken tofu
1/2 cup (125 ml) soy milk
1/2 cup (125 ml) thick coconut
  cream
125 g macadamia spread (see Note)
1/4 cup (90 g) honey
4 ripe lady finger bananas

2 mangoes, peeled and cut into
  1 cm cubes
1/2 cup (80 g) sultanas
1 teaspoon soy butter

1 Grease a 1.5 litre (8 x 8 x 22 cm) terrine dish with soy bean oil and line with baking paper. Sprinkle half the coconut over the base of the dish.
2 Blend the tofu, soy milk, coconut cream, macadamia spread, honey and bananas in a food processor until smooth.
3 Pour the tofu and banana mixture into the prepared dish and evenly spread the mango and sultanas on top—gently swirl with a knife to distribute evenly. Sprinkle the remaining coconut over the fruit.

Cover with plastic wrap and freeze for 8 hours, or overnight.
4 Just before serving, uncover the terrine and place in a sink of hot water for 1 minute, ensuring the water doesn't reach the top of the tin. Wipe the tin with a tea towel before you run a knife around the edges, then turn out onto a serving plate. Dip a sharp knife in hot water, slice and serve immediately.

NUTRITION PER SERVE
Protein 3 g; Fat 20 g; Carbohydrate 39 g; Dietary Fibre 5 g; Cholesterol 0 mg; 1420 kJ (340 cal)

COOK'S FILE
Note: Macadamia spread is available from health food stores.

Blend the tofu, soy milk, coconut cream, macadamia spread, honey and bananas.

Distribute the mango cubes and sultanas by gently swirling with a knife.

Loosen the sides by running a knife around the edges of the dish.

Soak the gelatine in water, then squeeze out any excess liquid.

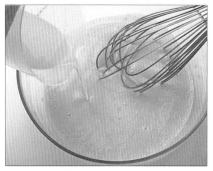

Whisk the remaining soy milk and vanilla into the tofu dessert mixture.

Pour the combined tofu dessert and soy milk mixtures through a fine sieve.

Cut the oranges into segments with a sharp knife.

SOY PANNA COTTA WITH ORANGE COMPOTE

Preparation time: 20 minutes +
  4 hours refrigeration
Total cooking time: 20 minutes
Serves 4

soy bean oil, for brushing
2 tablespoons caster sugar
1 cup (250 ml) creamy soy milk
1¼ gelatine leaves
150 g apricot tofu dessert
¼ teaspoon vanilla essence

Orange compote
2 oranges
¼ cup (60 g) caster sugar
1 cinnamon stick

1 Lightly grease four ¼ cup (60 ml) ramekins with the oil. Place the sugar and ⅔ cup (170 ml) of the soy milk in a saucepan. Stir over medium heat until the sugar has dissolved, then bring to the boil. Remove from the heat and set aside.
2 Cover the gelatine leaves with water in a small bowl and leave for 5 minutes, or until soft. Squeeze out any excess water. Add to the soy milk mixture and stir until dissolved. Leave to cool slightly.
3 Blend the tofu dessert in a food processor until smooth, then transfer to a bowl. Whisk in the soy milk mixture, then the vanilla essence and the remaining soy milk. Pour the mixture through a fine sieve. Pour into the prepared ramekins and refrigerate for at least 4 hours, or until set.
4 To make the orange compote, peel and segment the oranges over a bowl, to the catch the excess juice—reserve ¼ cup (60 ml) of the juice. Place the sugar in a small saucepan with the reserved juice, cinnamon stick and ¾ cup (185 ml) water. Bring to the boil and stir until the sugar dissolves. Reduce the heat and simmer for 10–12 minutes, or until it thickens slightly. Remove from the heat and sit for 5 minutes. Pour the syrup over the orange segments and leave to cool.
5 Carefully turn the panna cotta onto serving plates. Spoon some orange segments around each panna cotta and drizzle with a little of the extra syrup.

NUTRITION PER SERVE
Protein 5 g; Fat 13 g; Carbohydrate 30 g;
Dietary Fibre 1 g; Cholesterol 0 mg;
1014 kJ (242 cal)

DATE CUSTARD TART

Preparation time: 35 minutes +
20 minutes refrigeration
Total cooking time:
1 hour 40 minutes
Serves 8

1¼ cups (155 g) plain flour
80 g cold butter, chopped
60 g ground walnuts
2 tablespoons iced water
icing sugar, for dusting

Filling
130 g fresh dates
1 cup (250 ml) soy milk
½ vanilla bean
2 eggs
¼ cup (60 g) caster sugar

1 Sift the flour into a large bowl and add the butter. Rub the butter into the flour with your fingertips until it resembles fine breadcrumbs. Stir in the walnuts, then make a well in the centre. Add the iced water and mix with a flat-bladed knife, using a cutting action until the mixture comes together in small beads.
2 Gently gather the dough together into a ball and transfer to a sheet of baking paper. Roll out to fit a 22 cm loose bottomed fluted flan tin. Line the tin with the pastry, trim the edges and refrigerate for 20 minutes.
3 Preheat the oven to warm 170°C (325°F/Gas 3). Line the pastry shell with a sheet of baking paper large enough to cover the base and side of the tin and fill with baking beads or uncooked rice. Bake for 15 minutes, remove the paper and

beads, then bake for a further 20 minutes, or until the pastry is lightly golden and dry. Cool.
4 To make the filling, cut the dates into quarters lengthways and discard the stones. Arrange, cut-side-down, in circles on the pastry base. Pour the soy milk into a saucepan. Split the vanilla bean lengthways, scrape the seeds into the milk and add the bean. Slowly heat the soy milk until almost boiling.
5 Meanwhile, whisk the eggs and sugar together in a bowl. Slowly pour the hot milk onto the egg mixture, whisking gently as you pour. Discard the vanilla bean.
6 Place the tin on a flat baking tray. Gently pour the custard over the dates. Bake for 1 hour, or until the custard has set. Cool to room temperature, then dust with icing sugar before serving.

NUTRITION PER SERVE
Protein 6 g; Fat 16 g; Carbohydrate 35 g; Dietary Fibre 2.5 g; Cholesterol 70 mg; 1228 kJ (293 cal)

COOK'S FILE
Notes: Dates are the fruit of the palm tree and can be traced to the hot, dry desert regions of North Africa, the Middle East and India. Carvings dating back to early Egyptian and Mesopotamian civilisations often feature palm trees, also illustrating that dates were already used as a staple food.
Today, most dates are still grown in their regions of origin, with the biggest producers being from Egypt, Iraq, Iran and Saudi Arabia.
The Romans also liked dates, but had to import them from the East. Dates were used as a sweetener, or stuffed to make a sweetmeat.

Rub the butter into the flour with your fingers until it resembles breadcrumbs.

Mix the 'breadcrumb' mixture and water with a knife until it forms beads.

Line the flan tin with the pastry and trim the edges.

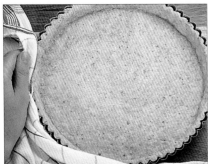

Bake the pastry, first filled with beans and then without, until it is dry.

Arrange the prepared dates, cut-side-down, on the pastry base.

Scrape the seeds from the split vanilla bean and add to the milk.

COFFEE SOY ICE CREAM WITH AMARETTO SYRUP

Preparation time: 20 minutes +
 35 minutes cooling +
 9 hours 30 minutes freezing
Total cooking time: 25 minutes
Serves 4

1½ cups (375 ml) coffee-flavoured
 soy milk
1 cup (250 ml) cream
1 teaspoon instant coffee
4 egg yolks
⅓ cup (90 g) sugar
50 g toasted flaked almonds

Amaretto syrup
⅓ cup (90 g) caster sugar
3 tablespoons Amaretto liqueur

1 Heat the soy milk and cream in a saucepan over low heat until just simmering. Remove from the heat and stir in the coffee until dissolved.
2 Beat the egg yolks and sugar with electric beaters for 2–3 minutes, or until light and creamy. Gradually whisk in the soy milk mixture. Return to the pan, stirring constantly for 5 minutes, or until thick enough to coat the back of a metal spoon and a line is left when you run a finger down the spoon. Remove from the heat and cool to room temperature.
3 Pour the mixture into a shallow metal tray. Cover with plastic wrap and freeze for 1 hour 30 minutes, or until half frozen. Blend the mixture in a food processor for 15 seconds, or until smooth. Return to the metal tray and freeze for at least 8 hours. Remove from the freezer 15 minutes before serving to allow it to soften.
4 To make the syrup, place the sugar in a small saucepan with ½ cup (125 ml) water, stirring constantly over low heat until the sugar has dissolved. Simmer for 8–10 minutes, or until syrupy. Remove from the heat and stir in the liqueur. Allow to cool, then drizzle generously over scoops of the ice cream. Garnish with almonds and serve immediately.

NUTRITION PER SERVE
Protein 9 g; Fat 42 g; Carbohydrate 60 g;
Dietary Fibre 1 g; Cholesterol 260 mg;
2652 kJ (633 cal)

Beat the egg yolks and sugar in a large bowl until light and creamy.

Check the consistency by running your finger along the back of a spoon.

Blend the half-frozen mixture in a food processor until smooth.

Simmer the water and sugar, stirring, until syrupy.

BAKED CUSTARDS WITH POACHED TAMARILLOS

Preparation time: 20 minutes
Total cooking time: 50 minutes
Serves 4

3 eggs
¼ cup (60 g) caster sugar
1 teaspoon vanilla essence
2 cups (500 ml) soy milk, warmed
1 tablespoon soft brown sugar

Poached tamarillos
4 tamarillos
1½ cups (375 g) caster sugar
1 cinnamon stick
4 cloves

1 Preheat the oven to warm 170°C (325°F/Gas 3). Place four ½ cup (125 ml) ramekin dishes in a deep baking tray.

2 Beat the eggs, sugar and vanilla in a large bowl. Gradually whisk in the soy milk, then strain through a fine sieve. Pour the milk mixture into the prepared ramekins, then pour enough boiling water into the baking tray until it comes halfway up the side of the ramekins.

3 Bake for 25 minutes, or until the custard is set and a skewer comes out clean when inserted in the centre. Evenly sprinkle the brown sugar on top and place under a hot grill for 2–3 minutes, or until the sugar melts and caramelises.

4 To make the poached tamarillos, place the tamarillos in a saucepan of boiling water and cook for 30 seconds. Drain, cool slightly and peel off the skin. Place the sugar, cinnamon, cloves and 3 cups (750 ml) water in the cleaned pan and stir over medium heat until the sugar has dissolved. Bring the syrup to the boil and cook for 3 minutes. Reduce the heat to a simmer, add the tamarillos and cook for 6–8 minutes. Turn off the heat and leave in the syrup to cool. Remove the fruit from the pan, then return the syrup to the heat. Boil for 5–10 minutes, or until thickened. Cool. Halve the tamarillos, leaving the stalk intact. Serve with hot or warmed syrup and the baked custard.

NUTRITION PER SERVE
Protein 9.5 g; Fat 8 g; Carbohydrate 122 g; Dietary Fibre 3.5 g; Cholesterol 135 mg; 2311 kJ (552 cal)

Whisk the warmed soy milk into the beaten egg and sugar mixture.

Strain the custard mixture through a fine sieve.

Briefly cook the tamarillos in boiling water, then peel off the skin.

BREAD AND BUTTER PUDDING

Preparation time: 20 minutes +
  10 minutes standing
Total cooking time: 50 minutes
Serves 6–8

10 slices soy and linseed bread
50 g soy butter
30 g sultanas
2 tablespoons orange marmalade,
  melted
3 eggs
3 cups (750 ml) vanilla-flavoured
  soy milk

1/3 cup (90 g) caster sugar
1/2 teaspoon ground cinnamon
1/2 teaspoon caster sugar, extra
icing sugar, for dusting

1 Preheat the oven to moderate
180°C (350°F/Gas 4). Grease a 2 litre
(26 x 16 x 5 cm) ovenproof dish.
Cut the crusts off the bread, then
spread with soy butter. Cut each
slice in half on the diagonal. Arrange
half the bread slices in the prepared
dish, buttered-side-up, then sprinkle
with half the sultanas. Layer with
the remaining slices and sprinkle
with the remaining sultanas. Add
1 tablespoon warm water to the
melted marmalade, then brush

liberally over the surface.
2 Whisk the eggs, soy milk and
sugar together, pour evenly over the
bread and leave for 10 minutes.
Combine the cinnamon and extra
sugar and sprinkle over the pudding.
3 Place the ovenproof dish in a deep
baking tin. Pour enough boiling
water into the baking tin until it
comes halfway up the sides. Bake for
50 minutes, or until the custard is set
and a skewer comes out clean when
inserted in the centre. Dust with icing
sugar and serve.

NUTRITION PER SERVE (8)
Protein 9.5 g; Fat 12 g; Carbohydrate 44 g;
Dietary Fibre 2 g; Cholesterol 68 mg;
1242 kJ (297 cal)

*Arrange half the buttered bread in the
dish and sprinkle with half the sultanas.*

*Liberally brush the marmalade over the
bread slices.*

*Place the dish in a deep baking tin and
half fill with boiling water.*

MANGO AND PASSIONFRUIT INDIVIDUAL TRIFLES

Preparation time: 20 minutes +
  soaking time
Total cooking time: 5 minutes
Serves 4

6 sponge finger biscuits
¼ cup (60 ml) vanilla-flavoured soy
  milk
2 mangoes, thinly sliced
170 g can passionfruit pulp in
  syrup

2 x 200 g tubs apricot soy yoghurt
1 tablespoon flaked almonds

1 Crumble the sponge finger biscuits into a small bowl. Pour the vanilla-flavoured soy milk over the biscuit crumbs and allow to soak up the liquid.
2 Spoon 2 tablespoons of the crumb mixture into each of four 300 ml glasses. Divide half the mango and passionfruit among the glasses, then top each with 2 tablespoons of the yoghurt. Repeat with the remaining crumbs, mango, passionfruit and yoghurt.
3 Spread the flaked almonds evenly onto the base of a dry frying pan. Toast gently over low heat, stirring occasionally, until golden.
4 To serve, sprinkle the individual trifles with the toasted almonds and chill until ready to serve.

NUTRITION PER SERVE
Protein 9 g; Fat 9 g; Carbohydrate 35 g;
Dietary Fibre 8.5 g; Cholesterol 0 mg;
1023 kJ (244 cal)

COOK'S FILE
Note: Four fresh passionfruit may be substituted for the canned pulp. Use half for the first layer and the other half for the top layer. Drizzle a little honey over the top of each one to sweeten.

Pour the soy milk over the crumbled sponge finger biscuits.

Spoon 2 tablespoons of the flavoured soy yoghurt into each serving glass.

Toast the almonds in a dry frying pan until golden.

CHOCOLATE TOFU CHEESECAKE

Preparation time: 20 minutes +
   6 hours refrigeration
Total cooking time: Nil
Serves 10

200 g chocolate-flavoured
   biscuits
90 g butter, melted
1 tablespoon gelatine
600 g silken tofu, drained
250 g soy cream cheese
1/2 cup (125 g) caster sugar
2 teaspoons vanilla essence
250 g dark chocolate, melted and
   cooled
2 tablespoons shaved chocolate
250 g strawberries, cut into quarters,
   to serve

1 Grease a 23 cm springform tin and line the base with non-stick baking paper.
2 Place the biscuits in a food processor and blend until finely crushed. Add the butter and process until combined. Spoon the biscuit mixture into the prepared tin and evenly smooth over the base with the back of a spoon. Refrigerate until required.
3 Meanwhile, sprinkle the gelatine evenly over 1/4 cup (60 ml) warm water in a small bowl. Leave until the gelatine is spongy—do not stir. Bring a small saucepan of water to the boil, remove from the heat and place the bowl in the pan. The water should come halfway up the side of the bowl. Stir the gelatine until clear and dissolved.
4 Place the tofu, soy cream cheese,

sugar, essence, melted chocolate and gelatine in a food processor and blend until smooth. Spoon the filling into the prepared tin and refrigerate for 6 hours, or until set.
5 Garnish with the shaved chocolate and serve with a generous pile of quartered strawberries.

NUTRITION PER SERVE
Protein 10 g; Fat 30 g; Carbohydrate 43 g; Dietary Fibre 1.24 g; Cholesterol 50 mg; 1964 kJ (469 cal)

COOK'S FILE
Note: Make one day in advance to improve flavour and texture. It will keep well for up to 4 days.

Blend the butter and finely crushed biscuits until well combined.

Soak the gelatine in warm water until it becomes spongy.

Blend all the filling ingredients in a food processor until the mixture is smooth.

PEACH CRUMBLE

Preparation time: 15 minutes
Total cooking time: 25 minutes
Serves 4

2 x 415 g cans sliced peaches,
    drained
½ cup (45 g) flaked almonds
⅓ cup (60 g) soft brown sugar
⅓ cup (35 g) rolled oats

½ teaspoon baking powder
½ cup (60 g) plain flour
⅓ cup (35 g) soy flour
½ teaspoon gluten flour
75 g soy butter, chopped
soy custard, to serve

1 Preheat the oven to moderate 180°C (350°F/Gas 4). Place the peach slices in a 15 x 24 cm ovenproof ceramic dish. Combine the almonds, brown sugar, oats and baking powder in a bowl.

2 Sift the flours into a bowl and add the chopped soy butter. Rub the butter into the flour with your fingertips until crumbly. Stir in the almond mixture and spoon evenly over the peaches. Bake for 25 minutes, or until lightly golden brown. Serve hot or warm with the soy custard.

NUTRITION PER SERVE
Protein 10 g; Fat 28 g; Carbohydrate 56 g; Dietary Fibre 6.5 g; Cholesterol 0 mg; 2143 kJ (512 cal)

Combine the almonds, sugar, oats and baking powder in a bowl.

Rub the soy butter into the flours with your fingertips until crumbly.

Spoon the crumble topping evenly over the peaches.

Pour the warmed milk into the egg mixture, stirring continuously.

Stir the milk and egg mixture over simmering water until it thickens.

Whisk the tofu through the milk and egg mixture until well combined.

SOY BAVAROIS WITH MIXED BERRIES

Preparation time: 20 minutes +
    4 hours refrigeration
Total cooking time: 10 minutes
Serves 4

soy bean oil, for greasing
2 egg yolks
1/4 cup (60 g) caster sugar
3/4 cup (185 ml) creamy soy milk
1 1/3 gelatine leaves
200 g berry tofu dessert, lightly
    beaten
250 g mixed fresh or frozen berries
    (blackberries, strawberries,
    raspberries, blueberries)
1 tablespoon caster sugar, extra

1 Lightly grease four 100 ml dariole moulds (see Note).
2 Combine the egg yolks and sugar in a heatproof bowl. Heat the soy milk in a small saucepan over medium heat until almost boiling. Gradually pour onto the egg mixture, stirring constantly as you pour. Place the bowl over a saucepan of simmering water, ensuring the bottom of the bowl doesn't touch the water, and stir for 10 minutes, or until it thickens and coats the back of a spoon.
3 Soak the gelatine in cold water for 1 minute, or until softened. Squeeze any excess water from the gelatine. Add the gelatine to the egg mixture and stir until dissolved. Place the bowl over iced water to chill, and whisk frequently. When cool, gently whisk in the tofu dessert until thoroughly combined. Pour into the prepared moulds and refrigerate for at least 4 hours, or until set.
4 Place the mixed berries in a saucepan with the extra sugar. Cook, stirring, over low heat for 3–5 minutes, or until the sugar has dissolved. Cool completely.
5 To serve, dip the dariole moulds in hot water for 3–5 seconds and turn out onto serving plates. Spoon the mixed berries and syrup around the bavarois and serve.

NUTRITION PER SERVE
Protein 9 g; Fat 20 g; Carbohydrate 32 g;
Dietary Fibre 1 g; Cholesterol 200 mg;
1323 kJ (316 cal)

COOK'S FILE
Note: Dariole moulds are metal moulds used for baked and steamed puddings or moulding set puddings and jellies. Available from speciality cookware stores.

APPLE PIE WITH CINNAMON SOY PASTRY

Preparation time: 30 minutes + refrigeration
Total cooking time: 45 minutes
Serves 4–6

1 cup (125 g) plain flour
1 cup (125 g) self-raising flour
1/3 cup (35 g) soy flour
75 g cold butter, chopped
75 g cold soy butter
1/4 cup (60 g) caster sugar
1 teaspoon ground cinnamon
1 egg
1 tablespoon caster sugar, extra

Filling

2 x 425 g cans pie apples
2 tablespoons caster sugar
1 tablespoon marmalade

1 Sift the flours into a bowl. Rub in the butter and soy butter with your fingertips until the mixture resembles fine breadcrumbs. Add the sugar and cinnamon. Make a well in the centre and stir in the egg and enough water to make a soft dough. Turn out onto a lightly floured surface and knead for 1 minute, or until smooth. Gather together into a ball and wrap in plastic wrap. Refrigerate for at least 1 hour.
2 To make the filling, place the apples, sugar and marmalade in a bowl and mix together well.
3 Divide the dough in half, making one portion a little larger than the other. Roll the larger piece of dough between two sheets of baking paper to fit a 25.5 cm pie dish. Fit the pastry into the pie dish and trim the edges. The pastry will be soft and it may be necessary to patch as you go.
4 Spread the filling evenly over the pastry base. Roll the remaining pastry between two sheets of baking paper and fit over the top of the apple filling. Trim off any excess pastry, then flute the edges. Make 2–3 small slashes in the pastry as steam vents. Decorate with pastry leaves, using any leftover pastry, if desired. Sprinkle the top with the extra sugar and refrigerate for 20 minutes.
5 Preheat the oven to moderately hot 200°C (400°F/Gas 6). Place a baking tray on the oven shelf. Put the pie dish on the hot tray and bake for 20 minutes. Reduce the heat to moderate 180°C (350°F/Gas 4) and bake for a further 20–25 minutes, or until the pastry is crisp and cooked. To prevent the edges from browning too much, cover with a large sheet of foil that has an 18 cm hole cut out of the centre. Serve the pie hot with soy custard or ice cream.

NUTRITION PER SERVE (6)
Protein 9 g; Fat 25 g; Carbohydrate 70 g; Dietary Fibre 4 g; Cholesterol 62 mg; 2260 kJ (540 cal)

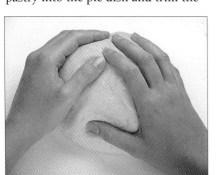

Briefly knead the dough, then bring it together into a ball.

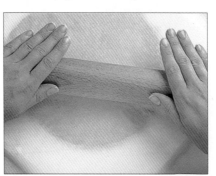

Roll the dough between two sheets of baking paper to fit the pie dish.

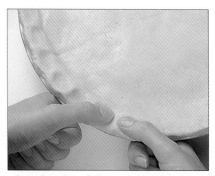

Flute the edge of the pie by gently pressing your thumbs into the dough.

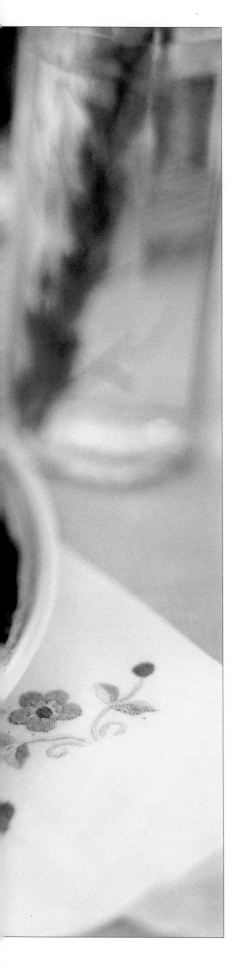

BAKING

CHOCOLATE SOY CAKE

Preparation time: 30 minutes +
  overnight chilling
Total cooking time:
  1 hour 30 minutes
Serves 8–12

Icing
3/4 cup (160 g) fructose
1/2 cup (60 g) cocoa powder
150 ml soy milk
1 teaspoon vanilla essence

2 1/4 cups (280 g) plain flour
3/4 cup (90 g) cocoa powder
1/2 teaspoon baking powder
1/2 teaspoon bicarbonate of soda
2 eggs
4 egg whites
2/3 cup (165 ml) soy milk
2 tablespoons instant coffee
  dissolved in 3 tablespoons
  hot water
1 teaspoon vanilla essence
240 g soy spread
3 cups (645 g) fructose
icing sugar, for dusting

1 To make the icing, combine the fructose and cocoa powder in a saucepan. Whisk in half the soy milk to form a smooth paste, then add the remaining soy milk. Bring to the boil over medium heat, then reduce the heat and simmer for 3 minutes—stir constantly with a wooden spoon. Remove from the heat and stir in the essence. Pour through a fine sieve and chill overnight.

2 Preheat the oven to moderate 180°C (350°F/Gas 4). Lightly grease a 3 litre bundt tin.

3 Sift the plain flour, cocoa, baking powder, bicarbonate of soda and 1/2 teaspoon salt into a large bowl. In a separate bowl, whisk the whole eggs and the egg whites until well mixed. Combine the soy milk, coffee and vanilla essence.

4 Cream the soy spread in a bowl using electric beaters, then gradually add the fructose. Beat on high speed for 2 minutes. Gradually add the egg mixture and beat for 3 minutes. Reduce the speed to low and add one third of the dry ingredients, scraping down the sides. Increase to medium speed and beat in half the soy milk mixture. Beat in the remaining dry ingredients alternately with the soy milk mixture until combined. Spoon into the prepared tin.

5 Bake for 1 hour 15 minutes to 1 hour 30 minutes, or until a skewer comes out clean when inserted into the centre of the cake. Cover the cake with foil halfway through if the surface begins to overbrown. Leave to cool in the tin. Turn out on a serving platter, dust with icing sugar and drizzle with the icing.

NUTRITION PER SERVE (12)
Protein 8 g; Fat 24 g; Carbohydrate 60 g;
Dietary Fibre 1.5 g; Cholesterol 30 mg;
2404 kJ (574 cal)

Whisk half the soy milk into the icing mixture to form a paste.

Beat in the remaining dry ingredients and soy milk until well combined.

SOY PECAN AND CINNAMON ROLLS

Preparation time: 35 minutes +
 1 hour 50 minutes rising
Total cooking time: 25 minutes
Makes 14

1 cup (250 ml) creamy soy milk
2 x 7 g sachets dried yeast
3 cups (375 g) plain flour
1 cup (120 g) soy flour
2 tablespoons gluten flour
1 tablespoon sugar
1/4 teaspoon soy bean oil
1/3 cup (115 g) soft brown sugar,
 firmly packed
2 teaspoons ground cinnamon
1 tablespoon soy spread, melted
1/2 cup (60 g) chopped pecans
1/2 cup (80 g) raisins

Maple glaze
1 1/2 tablespoons butter
3/4 cup (90 g) sifted icing sugar
1 1/2 tablespoons maple syrup
1 tablespoon milk

1 Warm 1/2 cup (125 ml) of the soy milk and 1/2 cup (125 ml) water in a small saucepan—do not boil. Transfer to a small bowl. Sprinkle the yeast over the surface and dissolve in the liquid. Leave in a warm place for 10 minutes, or until foamy. If your yeast doesn't foam it is dead and you will have to start again.
2 Combine the flours, sugar and 1 teaspoon salt in a large bowl and make a well in the centre. Add the yeast mixture and the remaining soy milk and mix until well combined. Turn out onto a lightly floured surface and knead for 1 minute, or until the dough forms a smooth ball—add a little extra plain flour if necessary.
3 Grease a large clean bowl with the oil, add the dough and turn to coat. Cover with a damp tea towel and leave to rise in a warm place for 1 hour, or until doubled in size.
4 Combine the brown sugar and cinnamon in a small bowl. Grease two baking trays with soy spread.
5 Turn the dough out onto a lightly floured surface and divide in half. Return one portion to the bowl and

cover. Roll out the other to a 24 cm square. Brush the dough with half the melted soy spread. Sprinkle half the cinnamon sugar mixture evenly on the dough, leaving a 1 cm border at the far end. Scatter half the pecans and half the raisins on top. Starting with the edge closest to you, roll up tightly and pinch along the far edge to secure the roll. Repeat with the remaining dough, soy spread and filling ingredients.
6 With the seam side down, cut each roll into 7 portions (about 3.5 cm wide). Place each portion on the prepared trays leaving a 3 cm gap between them. Cover with a tea towel

Sprinkle half the cinnamon sugar on the dough, leaving a border at the top.

and leave in a warm place to rise for 40 minutes. Preheat the oven to moderate 180°C (350°F/Gas 4). Bake for 20 minutes—cover with foil halfway through cooking to prevent over-browning. Cool on a wire rack.
7 To make the maple glaze, melt the butter in a small saucepan over low heat. Remove from the heat and stir in the icing sugar and maple syrup until dissolved, then stir in the milk. Drizzle the glaze over the rolls while still warm.

NUTRITION PER ROLL
Protein 7.5 g; Fat 8 g; Carbohydrate 44 g;
Dietary Fibre 3 g; Cholesterol 0 mg;
1126 kJ (270 cal)

Hold the roll, seam-side-down, and cut into seven even-sized portions.

SOY SCONES

Preparation time: 15 minutes
Total cooking time: 12 minutes
Makes 10

1½ cups (185 g) self-raising flour
½ cup (50 g) soy flour
1 teaspoon gluten flour
1 teaspoon baking powder
30 g cold soy butter, chopped
1 tablespoon caster sugar
¾ cup (185 ml) soy milk
soy milk, extra, for brushing

1 Preheat the oven to moderately hot 200°C (400°F/Gas 6). Lightly flour a baking tray.
2 Sift the self-raising, soy and gluten flours and baking powder into a large bowl. Rub the soy butter into the flours with your fingertips until evenly distributed. Stir in the sugar and make a well in the centre.
3 Add almost all the soy milk to the flour mixture and mix lightly with a flat-bladed knife to form a soft dough—add the remaining milk, if necessary. Knead the dough briefly on a lightly floured surface until smooth, then pat out to a 2 cm

thickness. Cut into rounds using a 4 cm scone cutter and place close together on the prepared baking tray. Gather the remaining dough together with your hands and repeat. Brush the tops of the scones with the extra soy milk. Bake for 10–12 minutes, or until golden brown. Serve with soy butter and marmalade or jam.

NUTRITION PER SCONE
Protein 3.5 g; Fat 4.5 g; Carbohydrate 17 g; Dietary Fibre 1.5 g; Cholesterol 0 mg; 500 kJ (120 cal)

With clean hands, rub the soy butter into the dry ingredients.

Mix with a flat-bladed knife to form a soft dough.

Pat the dough to a 2 cm thickness and cut into rounds with a scone cutter.

ITALIAN OLIVE AND THYME COUNTRY LOAF

Preparation time: 35 minutes +
  2 hours 25 minutes rising
Total cooking time: 45 minutes
Serves 8

1 teaspoon honey
1 teaspoon dry yeast
3 cups (375 g) plain flour
1/2 cup (50 g) soy flour
1/2 cup (125 ml) tepid soy milk
1/4 cup (35 g) wholemeal flour,
  for dusting
1 1/2 tablespoons fresh thyme,
  chopped
1/2 cup (80 g) pitted Kalamata olives,
  roughly chopped and squeezed dry
3 teaspoons soy bean oil
2 tablespoons fine cornmeal,
  for dusting

1 Place the honey and 1/3 cup (80 ml) warm water in a bowl and stir until the honey is dissolved. Sprinkle the yeast over the surface and stir until dissolved. Stand in a warm place for 10 minutes, or until the mixture is foamy. If your yeast doesn't foam, it is dead and you will have to start again.
2 Sift the plain and soy flours and 1 teaspoon salt into a deep bowl and make a well in the centre.
3 Stir the soy milk and 1/2 cup (125 ml) tepid water into the yeast mixture. Pour into the dry ingredients and incorporate the flour and liquid until it forms a ball. Dust a clean surface with the wholemeal flour and turn out the dough. Knead for 8 minutes, or until the dough is smooth and elastic and shaped into a tight ball.

4 Combine the thyme and olives, spread the mixture on the kneading surface, then roll the dough over the top. Gently knead for a further 2 minutes, incorporating the thyme and olives into the dough.
5 Grease a deep clean bowl with 2 teaspoons of the oil. Toss to coat and cover with a clean damp tea towel. Leave in a warm place for 1 hour 15 minutes, or until doubled in size. Punch down the dough and shape into a round.
6 Grease a round 22 cm cake tin, then dust the base and side with the cornmeal. Place the dough in the prepared cake tin. Brush the surface of the dough with the remaining oil. Cover with a damp tea towel and leave in a warm place for 1 hour, or until doubled in size.
7 Preheat the oven to moderately hot 200°C (400°F/Gas 6). Cut a couple of slashes (2 cm deep and 4 cm long) across the top of the loaf. Bake for 45 minutes, or until the loaf sounds hollow when tapped on the bottom. Cool on a wire cooling rack.

NUTRITION PER SERVE
Protein 8.5 g; Fat 5 g; Carbohydrate 40 g; Dietary Fibre 3.5 g; Cholesterol 0 mg; 1005 kJ (240 cal)

Knead the dough continuously until smooth and elastic.

Roll the dough over the thyme and olive mixture, then knead to combine.

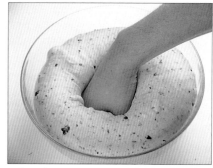

When the dough has doubled in size, punch down and shape into a round.

WHOLEMEAL ONION PULL-APART BREAD

Preparation time: 40 minutes +
  2 hours standing
Total cooking time: 50 minutes
Serves 8

7 g sachet dried yeast
1/2 teaspoon caster sugar
150 g silken tofu, at room
  temperature
1 tablespoon gluten flour
3²/3 cups (550 g) wholemeal flour
3 tablespoons soy bean oil
2 onions, cut into thin rings

1 Place the yeast, sugar and 1/2 cup
(125 ml) warm water in a small bowl.
Dissolve the yeast and allow to stand
for 8–10 minutes, or until frothy. If
your yeast doesn't foam it is dead and
you will have to start again. Combine
the tofu and 3/4 cup (185 ml) warm
water using a fork until smooth.
2 Place the gluten flour, 3¹/3 cups
(500 g) of the wholemeal flour and
1/2 teaspoon salt in a large bowl and
make a well in the centre. Add the
yeast and tofu mixtures to the dry
ingredients, mix with a wooden
spoon, then bring the dough together

with your hands. Turn out onto a
floured surface and knead for
7 minutes, or until smooth and
elastic—add the remaining flour,
as needed.
3 Grease a large bowl with a little
soy oil. Place the dough in the bowl
and brush the surface with oil. Cover
with a damp tea towel and stand for
1 hour, or until doubled in size.
4 Heat the remaining soy oil in a
frying pan. Add the onion and cook
over medium heat for 7–8 minutes,
or until very soft and golden. Drain
on paper towels. Allow to cool.
5 Grease a 9 x 25 cm bread tin and
line the base with baking paper.
Punch down the dough and knead
for a further 2 minutes. Divide the
dough into 8 even-size pieces. Form

each into 9 cm squarish pieces,
flattened slightly to 2 cm thick. Place
one square upright against one end
of the bread tin, tilt the tin, then
spread some of the onion on top.
Repeat with the remaining dough
and onion, finishing with a square of
dough. Cover with a damp tea towel
and leave for 45 minutes, or until
risen to almost the top of the tin.
6 Preheat the oven to moderately
hot 200°C (400°F/Gas 6). Bake for
35–40 minutes, or until golden
brown. Leave the bread in the tin
for 5 minutes, then turn out onto a
wire rack to cool.

NUTRITION PER SERVE
Protein 11 g; Fat 9.5 g; Carbohydrate 40 g;
Dietary Fibre 9 g; Cholesterol 0 mg;
1233 kJ (295 cal)

*Cook the onion rings in the soy oil until
very soft and golden.*

*Tilt the bread tin, then alternate the
dough with the onion mixture.*

103

SPICED SOY CRACKERS

Preparation time: 15 minutes +
 1 hour refrigeration
Total cooking time: 20 minutes
Makes 24

1¼ cups (155 g) plain flour
¾ cup (70 g) soy flour
½ teaspoon garam masala
½ teaspoon paprika
2½ tablespoons olive oil
2½ tablespoons lemon juice

1 Place the flours, garam masala, paprika and ½ teaspoon salt in a food processor. Add the oil, lemon juice and 100 ml water and blend until the mixture comes together in a ball. Cover in plastic wrap and place in the refrigerator for 1 hour.

2 Preheat the oven to warm 160°C (315°F/Gas 2–3). Line 3 baking trays with baking paper. Cut the dough into 5 or 6 pieces, then roll each piece into rectangles as thinly as possible—about 2 mm thick. Cut each piece into long thin triangles (4 x 10 cm). Place on prepared trays.

3 Bake for 20 minutes, or until crisp and lightly coloured. Serve with your favourite dip.

NUTRITION PER CRACKER
Protein 1.5 g; Fat 2 g; Carbohydrate 5.5 g; Dietary Fibre 0 g; Cholesterol 0 mg; 194 kJ (45 cal)

COOK'S FILE
Note: These crackers can be served with Soy bean hummus (page 33), Avocado and black bean salsa (page 33) or Fresh soy bean dip (page 35).

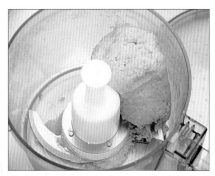

Blend the dry ingredients and the liquid until the mixture forms a ball.

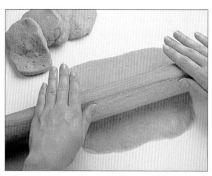

Roll each portion of dough into very thin rectangles.

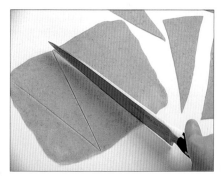

Using a sharp knife, cut long triangles from each rectangle.

CHOC CHIP COOKIES

Preparation time: 15 minutes
Total cooking time: 15 minutes
Makes 16

125 g soy butter
1 cup (185 g) soft brown sugar
1 teaspoon vanilla essence
1 egg, lightly beaten
1 tablespoon soy milk

1¼ cups (155 g) plain flour
½ cup (50 g) soy flour
1 teaspoon baking powder
250 g dark choc chips

1 Preheat the oven to moderate 180°C (350°F/Gas 4). Line a large baking tray with baking paper.
2 Cream the soy butter and sugar with electric beaters in a large bowl. Mix in the vanilla essence and gradually add the egg, beating well. Stir in the soy milk. Sift the flours and baking powder into a large bowl, then fold into the soy butter and egg mixture. Stir in the choc chips.
3 Drop level tablespoons of the cookie mixture onto the baking tray, leaving about 4 cm between each cookie, then lightly press with a floured fork. Bake for 15 minutes, or until lightly golden. Cool on a wire rack.

NUTRITION PER COOKIE
Protein 3.5 g; Fat 14 g; Carbohydrate 33 g; Dietary Fibre 1 g; Cholesterol 11 mg; 1090 kJ (260 cal)

Add the egg to the creamed butter and sugar, beating well.

Mix the choc chips into the dough until the ingredients are well incorporated.

Press down on the cookies with a lightly floured fork.

HERBED SOY AND LINSEED MUFFINS

Preparation time: 15 minutes
Total cooking time: 25 minutes
Makes 12

soy bean oil, for greasing
1½ cups (185 g) self-raising flour
¾ cup (90 g) soy flour
¾ cup (100 g) ground LSA (see Note)
2 tablespoons chopped fresh chives
2 tablespoons chopped fresh parsley
1 cup (250 ml) soy milk
2 eggs
125 g soy spread, melted and cooled

1 Preheat the oven to moderately hot 200°G (400°F/Gas 6). Lightly grease twelve ½ cup muffin holes.
2 Sift the self-raising and soy flours into a large bowl, then stir in the LSA. Season well. Stir in the herbs, then make a well in the centre. Whisk the milk and eggs together in a jug, add to the dry ingredients with the melted soy spread and gently fold together with a metal spoon. Do not overmix—the batter should be lumpy. Overmixing will produce tough muffins.
3 Fill each muffin hole three-quarters full with the mixture. Bake for 20–25 minutes, or until golden brown and firm to the touch. Allow to cool for a couple of minutes, then gently loosen each muffin with a flat-bladed knife and lift out onto a wire rack. Delicious served warm with soup or with casseroles.

NUTRITION PER MUFFIN
Protein 7 g; Fat 18 g; Carbohydrate 13 g; Dietary Fibre 2.5 g; Cholesterol 30 mg; 980 kJ (234 cal)

COOK'S FILE
Note: LSA is a mixture made from ground linseed, sunflower seeds and almonds. It is available from the health food section of most supermarkets, or from health food stores.

Roughly chop the parsley and chives with a sharp knife.

Stir the LSA mixture into the sifted flours, then season.

SOY FRUIT MUFFINS

Preparation time: 20 minutes
Total cooking time: 30 minutes
Makes 6 large muffins

1/2 cup (50 g) soy flour, sifted
3/4 cup (75 g) rye flour, sifted
1/2 cup (80 g) brown rice flour, sifted
3/4 cup (75 g) rolled oats
2 1/2 teaspoons baking powder
1/2 cup (125 g) caster sugar
1 egg
3 tablespoons soy bean oil

1 1/2 cups (375 ml) soy milk
1/2 cup (95 g) chopped dried dates
1/2 cup (60 g) chopped dried bananas
1/3 cup (60 g) chopped dried figs
dried figs, chopped, extra, to garnish

1 Preheat the oven to moderate 180°C (350°F/Gas 4). Lightly grease six 1 cup muffin holes.
2 Place the soy, rye and brown rice flours, oats, baking powder and sugar in a bowl, then make a well in the centre. Whisk the egg, oil and soy milk in a jug and add to the dry ingredients. Add the dried dates, bananas and figs and fold gently with

a metal spoon until just combined. Do not overmix—the batter should be lumpy. Overmixing will produce tough muffins.
3 Fill each muffin hole two-thirds full with the mixture. Top with an extra piece of dried fig. Bake for 30 minutes, or until the muffins come away slightly from the sides of the tin. Allow to cool for a couple of minutes, then lift out onto a wire rack to cool with a flat-bladed knife.

NUTRITION PER MUFFIN
Protein 9.5 g; Fat 16 g; Carbohydrate 63 g; Dietary Fibre 6 g; Cholesterol 30 mg; 1712 kJ (409 cal)

Add the egg, oil and soy milk mixture to the dry ingredients.

Gently fold the dried fruit into the muffin mixture with a metal spoon.

Spoon the mixture into the muffin holes, filling them two-thirds full.

107

SOY BROWNIES

Preparation time: 15 minutes
Total cooking time: 30 minutes
Makes 24

1 cup (125 g) plain flour
1/2 cup (50 g) soy flour
1 teaspoon baking powder
1/3 cup (40 g) carob or cocoa
  powder
1/2 cup (60 g) chopped pecans
125 g butter, chopped
250 g soy chocolate, broken into
  pieces

1 cup (185 g) soft brown sugar
150 g silken firm tofu
2 eggs, lightly beaten
icing sugar, for dusting

1 Preheat the oven to moderate 180°C (350°F/Gas 4). Lightly grease a shallow 20 x 30 cm baking tin and line with enough baking paper to overlap on the longer sides—this will help when removing the brownies from the tin after cooking.
2 Sift the flours, baking powder and carob into a large bowl. Add the pecans and make a well in the centre.
3 Place the butter, soy chocolate and brown sugar in a heatproof bowl.

Place over a saucepan of simmering water, stirring frequently until the butter and chocolate have melted and combined. Set aside to cool slightly.
4 Mash the tofu well with a potato masher or fork and add to the dry ingredients. Add the eggs and the melted chocolate mixture and mix well with a metal spoon or a spatula. Pour the mixture into the prepared tin and bake for 25 minutes, or until firm. Cool in the tin. To serve, cut into slices and dust with icing sugar.

NUTRITION PER BROWNIE
Protein 2.5 g; Fat 8 g; Carbohydrate 15 g; Dietary Fibre 0 g; Cholesterol 28 mg; 577 kJ (138 cal)

Stir the butter, chocolate and sugar over simmering water until melted.

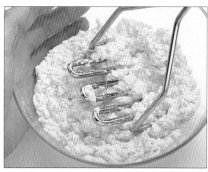

Mash the tofu with a potato masher in a small bowl.

Mix the tofu, eggs, chocolate mixture and dry ingredients until well combined.

COCONUT PINE SLICE

Preparation time: 20 minutes
Total cooking time: 40 minutes
Makes 24 pieces

¹/₃ cup (20 g) shredded coconut
³/₄ cup (90 g) self-raising flour
¹/₂ cup (50 g) soy flour
³/₄ cup (140 g) soft brown sugar
2 tablespoons sunflower seeds
2 tablespoons sesame seeds
¹/₂ cup (70 g) chopped
    macadamias
¹/₃ cup (60 g) chopped dates
1 tablespoon chopped glacé
    ginger
¹/₂ cup (45 g) desiccated coconut
³/₄ cup (230 g) canned crushed
    pineapple, drained
100 g soy spread or margarine,
    melted
2 eggs, lightly beaten

Icing
2 cups (250 g) icing sugar
30 g soy spread, melted
1¹/₂ tablespoons lemon juice

1 Preheat the oven to warm 170°C (325°F/Gas 3). Spread the coconut evenly on a baking tray and toast for 5–8 minutes, or until lightly golden. Grease a 20 x 30 cm shallow baking tin and line with enough baking paper to overlap on the longer sides—this will make the slice easier to remove once baked.
2 Sift the self-raising and soy flours into a large bowl. Add the brown sugar, seeds, macadamias, dates, ginger and desiccated coconut. Stir in the pineapple, melted soy spread and beaten egg and mix well.

3 Spoon the mixture into the prepared tin. Bake for 25–30 minutes, or until golden brown. Cool in the tin, remove and cover with the icing.
4 To make the icing, combine the icing sugar, melted soy spread and lemon juice in a small bowl. Stir in 1–2 teaspoons of boiling water to reach a smooth consistency. Spread evenly over the slice. Sprinkle the top

with the toasted shredded coconut and when set, slice and serve.

NUTRITION PER PIECE
Protein 2.5 g; Fat 11 g; Carbohydrate 22 g; Dietary Fibre 1.5 g; Cholesterol 15 mg; 8.3 kJ (192 cal)

COOK'S FILE
Note: Use other nuts or seeds, such as pumpkin seeds or almonds, if desired.

Toast the coconut on a baking tray until lightly golden.

Spoon the slice mixture into the prepared baking tin.

Mix all the icing ingredients together with a little boiling water until smooth.

109

CITRUS AND SOY YOGHURT CAKE

Preparation time: 25 minutes +
  20 minutes standing
Total cooking time: 1 hour
Serves 8

200 g soy butter
1 cup (250 g) caster sugar
2 teaspoons grated lemon rind
4 eggs, separated
2¼ cups (280 g) plain flour
⅓ cup (35 g) soy flour
1 teaspoon baking powder
1 teaspoon bicarbonate of soda
200 g vanilla soy yoghurt

Lemon syrup
2 teaspoons grated lemon rind
1 large strip lemon rind
½ cup (125 ml) lemon juice
¾ cup (185 g) caster sugar
1 fresh lemon leaf, optional

1 Preheat the oven to moderate 180°C (350°F/Gas 4). Lightly grease a 22 cm springform tin and line the base with baking paper. Beat the soy butter, sugar and lemon rind with electric beaters until light and creamy. Add the egg yolks one at a time, beating well after each addition. Transfer to a large bowl.
2 Sift the flours, baking powder and bicarbonate of soda together and fold into the creamed mixture in thirds, alternately with the soy yoghurt.
3 Beat the egg whites with electric beaters until firm (but not stiff) peaks form. Fold a large spoonful of egg white into the cake mixture to soften, then gently fold in the remaining egg white until incorporated.

4 Spoon into the tin and smooth the surface. Bake for 50 minutes, or until a skewer comes out clean when inserted into the centre of the cake. Cover with foil during the last 15 minutes if the surface is browning too much. Leave in the tin and place on a metal tray. Insert small holes all over the surface of the cake with a thin skewer.
5 To make the lemon syrup, combine the lemon rinds and juice, sugar, lemon leaf and ¼ cup (60 ml) water in a small saucepan. Stir over

low heat until the sugar is dissolved. Boil without stirring, for 10 minutes, or until thick and syrupy. Remove the lemon strip and lemon leaf and reserve. Pour the hot syrup over the warm cake and leave for 20 minutes to allow the syrup to absorb. Gently remove from the tin and serve with cream. If desired, garnish with the reserved lemon strip and leaf.

NUTRITION PER SERVE
Protein 9.5 g; Fat 30 g; Carbohydrate 83 g;
Dietary Fibre 2 g; Cholesterol 94 mg;
2618 kJ (625 cal)

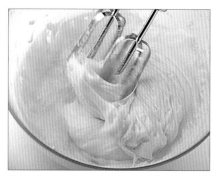

Beat the soy butter, sugar and lemon rind until light and creamy.

Beat the egg whites until firm (but not stiff) peaks form.

Gently fold the egg white into the cake mixture.

INDEX

INTERNATIONAL GLOSSARY OF INGREDIENTS

capsicum	red or green pepper	fresh coriander	fresh cilantro
eggplant	aubergine	tomato purée (Aus.)	sieved crushed tomatoes/ passata (UK)
tomato paste (Aus.)	tomato purée, double concentrate (UK)	zucchini	courgette

Published by Murdoch Books®, a division of Murdoch Magazines Pty Limited, GPO Box 1203, Sydney NSW 1045.

Managing Editor: Rachel Carter **Editor:** Stephanie Kistner **Creative Director:** Marylouise Brammer **Designer:** Michelle Cutler **Food Director:** Jane Lawson **Food Editor:** Melita Smilovic **Recipe Development:** Judy Clarke, Michelle Earl, Vicky Harris, Katy Holder, Jane Lawson, Valli Little, Nadine McCristal, Kerrie Mullins, Kate Murdoch, Sally Parker, Tracy Rutherford, Claudio Sherbini, Melita Smilovic **Home Economists:** Alison Adams, Ross Dobson, Justine Johnson, Anna Phillips, Angela Tregonning, Wendy Quisumbing **Photographers:** Rob Reichenfeld, Reg Morrison (steps) **Food Stylist:** Cherise Koch **Food Preparation:** Valli Little **Nutritionist:** Thérèse Abbey **UK Consultant:** Maggi Altham **CEO & Publisher:** Anne Wilson.

The nutritional information provided for each recipe does not include garnishes or accompaniments, such as rice, unless they are included in specific quantities in the ingredients. The values are approximations and can be affected by biological and seasonal variations in food, the unknown composition of some manufactured foods and uncertainty in the dietary database. Nutrient data given are derived primarily from the NUTTAB95 database produced by the Australian New Zealand Food Authority.

National Library of Australia Cataloguing-in-Publication Data. Cooking with soy. Includes index. ISBN 0 86411 9986 0. 1. Cookery (Soybeans). 2. Vegetarian cookery. 3. Soyfoods. I. Title: Family circle (Sydney, N.S.W.). 641.65655. First printed 2001.

Spice Girls

Publishing Director: **Laura Bamford**
Executive Editor: **Mike Evans**
Editor: **Humaira Husain**
Production Controller: **Mark Walker**
Picture Research: **Maxine McCaghy**
Art Director: **Keith Martin**
Design: **Geoff Borin**

First published in 1997 by
Hamlyn, an imprint of
Reed Consumer Books Limited,
Michelin House, 81 Fulham Road,
London SW3 6RB
and Auckland, Melbourne, Singapore and Toronto

A Catalogue record for this book is available from the British Library
ISBN 0 600 59255 3

Printed and bound in Great Britain by
Butler & Tanner Ltd, Frome and London

Spice Girls

PAUL LESTER

HAMLYN

Contents

Welcome back from Mars
if you haven't heard of
the Spice Girls. They're
the all-girl group who got
to Number 1 in the charts
in late summer 1996
with their debut single
'Wannabe

Wannabe Starlets

Although Spice Girls might seem like the brightest new girls on the block, they are most definitely not overnight sensations. In fact, they were working hard for three years before fame and fortune came knocking – the girls had been trying to get a break well after they left their stage schools and performing arts schools for wannabe singers, dancers and actresses.

WHO ARE THE SPICE GIRLS?

They're five normal English girls – Melanie 'Mel B' Brown, Geraldine 'Geri' Halliwell, Emma Bunton, Victoria 'Vicki' Addams and Melanie 'Mel C' Chisholm – with normal dreams of megastardom, who spent the latter years of their teens on the fringes of showbusiness.

How did they meet? There are two versions of Spice Girls' pre-history. One version has it that their paths crossed many times in the early Nineties at various studios and assorted locations. Victoria and Geri met at an audition for the *Tank Girl* film. Mel B and Mel C also ran into each other at auditions and at hip nightclubs. Then they all got to know Emma.

Version two of their early days suggests the five girls met via an advert in 'Luvvie Bible' *The Stage* (where theatrical/artistic types search for work on commercials, on the chorus lines of London musicals, and so forth), which was placed in the magazine on February 24th 1994.

According to a feature on BBC2's *The Sunday Show* which was aired on December 1st 1996, the advert was worded thus:-

'WANNABE STARLETS. RU 18-23 WITH THE ABILITY TO SING/DANCE? RU STREETWISE, OUTGOING, AMBITIOUS AND DEDICATED? HEART MANAGEMENT LTD ARE CURRENTLY FORMING A CHOREOGRAPHED, SINGING/DANCING, ALL-FEMALE POP ACT FOR A RECORDING ACT. OPEN AUDITION, DANCE WORKS, 16 BALDERTON STREET, FRIDAY 4TH MARCH.'

Out of 400 hopefuls, five were chosen. They became close friends, and soon they were dreaming of starting their *own* pop group.

And then, because two of them were out of work and two were constantly having to commute from up north, they decided to live together, just like The Monkees or The Beatles in *Help!*

Reports state that the girls spent nine months living together in a run-down, two-bedroom flat, before they moved to a

Mel B

Mel C

It was during an aerobics class that Geri had a flash of inspiration: they should call themselves Spice (*The Sunday Show* suggested it was actually a producer from the local studio, Tim Hawes, who came up with the name 'Spice Girls' when they recorded a track together called 'Sugar And Spice'. 'You're a spicy bunch,' he told them. 'How's about that for name?').

Unfortunately, a rapper called Spice had already beaten them to it, so Geri changed it to Spice Girls.

At the same time, the girls also realised it would be advantageous to exploit the endless possibilities of their different personalities and personal styles. They swore there and then never to be a boring teen group with the same clothes and the same dance routines.

Hence, Mel C became crystallised in her role as 'the sporty one', Vicki became 'the posh one', Geri 'the sexy one', Mel B 'the wild one' and Emma 'the cute one' – each persona was merely a slightly more exaggerated version of their real-life selves.

'There is something for everyone,' Vicki said, responding to accusations that the Spice Girls' five characters were ruthlessly contrived. 'But people should realise that's just the way we are.'

Geri

Emma

comparatively luxurious suburban house, either in Knaphill, Guildford, or in Maidenhead, Berkshire, or in Maidstone, Kent. The two Mels shared a bedroom, Vicki and Emma shared another, while Geri, the eldest, had her own.

They decided to devote all their spare time to writing and rehearsing down at the local studios, where, according to *The Sunday Show*, the Girls would 'slam their bodies down and wind them all around till their little Spice legs would drop off,' a wry reference to the lyrics of Spice Girls' first hit, 'Wannabe'.

At night, the girls would perform song-and-dance routines in front of their bedroom mirrors and began writing the 30-or-so songs that would lay the foundations for the Spice Girls' repertoire.

But they were yet to be known as Spice Girls – in fact, at that time they didn't have any name as such.

Vicki

The Gossip

In an interview given abroad, the girls confirm that they have lied about their ages.

Geri once pulled down her bikini bottom in front of a journalist, 'so he could see I'm not a natural red-head.'

Mel B has a pierced tongue. Says Geri: 'When she got it done, she wanted to know what it felt like, so she practised snogging on us!'

Geri doesn't believe that any of the Girls are sex goddesses, nor do they aim to be. In fact, 'we fart and burp and puke up when we're drunk — just like anyone else! That's why we treat everybody just the same, because everybody wees and everybody dies.'

Jarvis Cocker of Pulp is dying to team up with the girls for a recording session. The famous five have already written a song especially for him, but are too much in awe of their idol to even approach him. Says Jarvis: 'I've heard about this rumour, but they've not talked to me about it. Get in touch! It could be just what I need to revive my flagging career. Can you please give me their phone number?'

Geri fancies Tommy Scott from Scallydelic band Space, although the feeling isn't mutual. 'I've had the same girlfriend for 10 years, and I'm not about to change her now,' Tommy told *Melody Maker*. Sorry, Geri, you can't get what you want, what you really, really want, this time.

The ITN news reader Trevor MacDonald likes Spice Girls because they once sang him the theme tune to News At 10.

When the girls mounted a bronze statue of legendary horse Red Rum at Kempton Park racecourse, flashing their knickers and yelling, 'I'll tell you what I want, what I really, really want,' they had to be manhandled to the ground by burly stewards.

KNOWN AS: Sporty Spice

REAL NAME: Melanie Jayne Chisholm
('It sounds like jism')

NICKNAME AT SCHOOL: Holland
('because it's such a flat country')

AGE: 21

BIRTHDAY: 12th January 1976

STARSIGN: Capricorn

BIRTHPLACE: Widnes, near Liverpool

MUM AND DAD: Joan O'Neill, a secretary,
and stepdad Den (her real dad, William,
split with Joan when Mel was little)

EYES: Hazelnut brown

HAIR: Light brown

CLOTHES: Sportswear – Kappa, Adidas
and Umbro

LOVES: Football and Chinese food; Jamie
Rednapp and Steve McManaman from LFC

HATES: Smoking

MOST SEXY MAN: Bruce Willis

MUSIC: Neneh Cherry (when she was 15,
Mel C apparently believed she was
Neneh Cherry!)

FAVE TV SHOW: Brookside

WORST MOMENT: At the end of a Liverpool
game, they played 'Wannabe'

BAD HABIT: Uses men's loos

TATTOO/PIERCING: A 'dead cool' Celtic chain
tattoo round her left arm; she also has a
pierced nose

WISH: For Liverpool to win everything

HEROINES: Madonna and Neneh Cherry

BEST PICK-UP LINE: 'What's your favourite
football club?'

'SPORTY SPICE'

Mel C is the tomboy of the group, the one that kids like. She is quiet and headstrong, the strong and silent type. She may be shy, but she's definitely very healthy and sporty – she's the Spice Girl most likely to make it onto *Gladiators!*

Fit and funky she may be, but she's really just a girly underneath the tough exterior, a confirmed ballet fanatic who hates wearing tracksuits and trainers. One friend who lives near Mel's small, terraced home in Widnes, Cheshire, recently said: 'I saw her two weeks ago and she looked nothing like her Spice Girls image. She looks more feminine than ever.' Mel C is disciplined and diplomatic, and is also the only one of the group who doesn't smoke.

She almost got a part in the musical *Cats*, and was a contender for the lead role in the film *Tank Girl*. These days, she plays in the Rickmansworth Ladies' Football Club, and is obsessed with shopping for food! 'I can't get enough of it,' she says. 'When we have a day off, I'm straight down there. Sainsbury's, Tesco's – you name it!'

As a child, Mel devoted every Saturday to dancing lessons and always loved performing in school plays. Recalls a friend: 'She was a very good actress but she was known for her singing. Mel just wanted to perform in any way she could. She was destined to be famous.'

Childhood acquaintances believe she inherited her talent from her mum, and from the fact that her mum and stepdad have for years toured the clubs with their band T-Junction. Said Mel's school pal Zoe Curlett: 'Her mum is with the band every weekend. She has a terrific voice and it's obvious where Mel gets it from.'

After leaving school, Mel moved to Sidcup, Kent, to study ballet and jazz at the Doreen Bird dance school. She auditioned for plays and musicals until the chance came to join the Spice Girls.

But success hasn't spoiled her – according to neighbours, she's still the down-to-earth girl she always was: 'She's really close to her mum,' said one. 'And the day after the Japan tour finished, Mel left the others and headed straight home. She invited all the kids in from the street and posed for pictures with them. Mel is such a lovely girl. You can't help but like her.'

'I want people to think of us as the new Oasis'

Mel C – disciplined and diplomatic

'Five Lively Girls'

Mel B shows off her pierced tongue while Geri has a zig-a-zig-ah!

Being so different, and spending so much time together, caused a few problems, notably between the headstrong Geri and fiercely outspoken Mel B, who reputedly argued quite often back then (actually, they still do, which occasionally leads to vicious little catfights).

SpiceGirls

TWO EXTREMES

We've got two extremes of people in this group,' said Mel C. 'Those who don't like to say what they think, and those who do.'

Added Geri: 'People say I'm the bossy one, and that's basically because I am. I'm the organiser.'

No wonder there was tension in those early days. Because, to be frank, at this point Spice Girls were hardly the consummately professional, all-singing, all-dancing pop troupe they are today.

'Were they always fantastically talented?' asked a reporter on the December 1st edition of *The Sunday Show* in an interview with Ian Lee, who apparently knew the five girls back in their Knaphill days. 'No, not really,' was the reply.

The Sunday Show then showed some rehearsal footage of Vicki singing a standard show-tune rather badly.

Said Lee over the footage: 'In the beginning they couldn't sing very well.'

Then there was film of Mel B offering a rather shaky rendition of George Benson's 'The Greatest Love Of All'.

Added Lee, humorously, offscreen: 'And they couldn't even dance. . .'

Cue a screechy version of 'I'm So Excited' by The Pointer Sisters, courtesy of Mel C.

TOUGH TIMES

Around this period, a hapless entrepreneur advertised for 'five lively girls' – a greed-inspired idea which failed dismally after he chose Geri and Co, who were infact five extremely wilful young women and wise beyond their years.

He wanted them to be the perfect girl group, all matching outfits and docile demeanour, a Supremes or Ronettes for the Nineties, or the new Bananarama, the pop-dance trio who sold 10 million records in the Eighties. The girls, however, had other plans.

Reminiscing about those tough early times when it seemed as though the world and his wife wanted them to go against their natural inclinations, Vicki told *Select* magazine: 'It was really difficult. We had people saying, "You have to have a lead singer, and you've got to all dress the same, or it's not going to work." It's good for us that it did work, though, because we didn't want to change. We wanted to be ourselves and have a good time doing it.'

CREATIVE JUICES

The girls lived poorly throughout this period. 'We'd get taken out to dinner by record companies and we'd nick all the toilet rolls from the loos,' joked Mel C. 'We'd order loads and stuff our faces, and then we'd leave with half the table in our pockets'. Vicki: 'We felt like rejects, but we really got on well together. It just took off from there.'

Meanwhile, their creative juices flowed, and armed with a batch of effervescent dance-pop tunes, the girls headed for London in the time-honoured search for fame and fortune – and dumped their management on the way.

'They wanted a future,' said the screen presenter on *The Sunday Show*, slyly parodying the words to 'Wannabe', 'so they forgot their past. . .'

'The bloke wanted us to sing someone else's songs,' explained Mel C, summing up their understandable antipathy towards being manipulated and controlled by men. 'About love, and all that shit.'

After briefly managing themselves, they looked for a new manager, one who would ultimately get the girls the record contract they deserved.

HISTORY

The rest, as they say, is history (and hysteria for the numerous record companies that, convinced the last thing the boyband-obsessed world wanted was an all-girl group, turned the girls down, just as Decca Records had 30 years earlier turned down the opportunity to sign a raw new Liverpudlian band called The Beatles).

After six months of recording, the girls started turning up unannounced at record companies to sing *a capella* to bosses, marching into TV stations, and grabbing journalists for impromptu performances of their new material.

Mel B and Mel C: spicy Geisha Girls

Emma and Vicki: roommates in the early days

'We just set out on a mission to get exactly what we wanted,' recalled Mel B. 'We stormed into parties, sang in people's offices, did the lot. Then we'd sit at home and wait for them all to ring us up. And they did!' And then?

Emma: 'And then we set up a showcase at Nomis Studios using money put up by our parents. About 20 publishers came along and we waited for the deal to suit us.'

SPICE POWER

In May 1995, a demo (demonstration) tape of their recordings ended up at the offices of Simon Fuller, boss of 19 Management, whose clients include Annie Lennox and Cathy Dennis. And in true Spice style they invaded his office and convinced him that *he* should be the one to make them stars.

'Simon was really cool,' said Mel B. 'We had so many managers saying, "Dress like this, sing that song, I can make you big stars." Simon was really laidback and understood that we wanted a say in how our careers would go.'

Together, they got a publishing deal with Windswept Pacific, then met up with various record companies, launching their attack with some songs they'd been writing with Elliot C Kennedy (who has also co-written with Gary Barlow). They'd meet all the record company big-wigs and frighten the living daylights out of them with their over-the-top in-yer-face manner.

Said Geri: 'We liked Virgin because they offered us the chance to go our own way. We feel as though we're breaking down barriers, as women going up against the boy groups and people's expectations. There's more to us than a lot of those acts.'

There was *some* initial unease about signing Spice Girls, at a label whose roster of acts included the likes of Meat Loaf, Iggy Pop and Massive Attack. Virgin had long been the home of weird, leftfield stars, not all-girl mainstream swingbeat/rap posses. But there was a realisation that Virgin needed to expand their repertoire, and it was also clear that Spice Girls had credibility, as well as an irrepressible refreshing spirit of female camaraderie.

And so the Spice Girls signed to Virgin, who were determined to make Spice Power the globe's most formidable pop force.

To celebrate the deal, the girls insisted that Vicki get drunk on champagne. She got so paralytic, they ripped her knickers off and threw them out of a speeding taxi window.

The Rumours

The Spice Girls are the favourite group of Sarah 'Fergie' Ferguson, The Duchess of York

Mel B being saucy as usual

They urinated in some plant pots at the luxurious Four Seasons hotel in Los Angeles

At the aforementioned Four Seasons hotel, Emma streaked around the corridors with her dressing gown wide open, while Mel B and Geri mooned at the guests around the swimming pool

When they signed to Virgin, they sent along five blow-up dolls to the signing, then proceeded to chuck them off the 15th floor balcony of a hotel

A naked Pakistani transvestite act once sang Norman Greenbaum's 'Spirit In The Sky' to them

They've been offered one million pounds each to strip for a British TV show

The Girls go wild for Chris Evans

They abused Elton John and touched up Ulrika Jonsson at the 1996 Brit Awards, pinching the latter's backside

On the way to interview Spice Girls for a music paper, a journalist was warned by his cab driver, 'You'll never make it back alive!'

KNOWN AS: Sexy Spice or Ginger Spice

REAL NAME: Geri 'Geraldine' Halliwell

NICKNAME AT SCHOOL: None

NAME IF BORN A BOY: Freaky Fred

AGE: 24

BIRTHDAY: August 6th 1972

STARSIGN: Leo

BIRTHPLACE: Watford, Herts

MUM AND DAD: Anna Maria, who is Spanish (Geri is also one-quarter Swedish), Lawrence, a motor dealer in Watford

HOME: Geri lives in north London, near James Dean Bradfield of Manic Street Preachers

SCHOOL: Watford Grammar (where she was very popular)

EYES: Blue

HAIR: Red

CLOTHES: Anything 'crazy' (for example, the shiny black patent leather outfit she wore in the video for 'Say You'll Be There')

LOVES: Strong women; Hamlet cigars

MOST SEXY MAN: Noel Gallagher

WORST MOMENT: When I showed my Malcolm X walk in a restaurant

BAD HABIT: She always leaves the door open when taking a leak

TATTOO/PIERCING: A tattoo of a tiger on her arm; she's got a pierced belly-button and pierced ears

WISH: An Aston Martin DB6

HERO: Malcolm X ('for what he stood for') and Maggie Thatcher ('because she was the first woman ever in the government')

FAVE TV SHOW: Happy Days

MUSIC: Elvis Presley, Sneaker Pimps, Portishead and Space ('The singer's really sexy')

BEST PICK-UP LINE: 'Here's 10p, call your mum and tell her you won't be coming home tonight'

'SEXY SPICE'

Geri is a former wild child who is wise beyond her years. She speaks, in that inimitable husky voice of hers, more than the other Spice Girls in interviews.

She's a bit of a New Age Nineties hippychick who loves Seventies hot pants and thigh-high boots. She is, like Mel B, completely barmy and outgoing, and clearly doesn't know the meaning of the word 'embarrassment'.

Her period as a teen fitness freak had a considerable effect on men as she worked out in her skimpy outfits. A friend from her keep fit years recalled: 'She was always proud of her body and would train so she looked good. She was always taking classes and lifting weights. She caused a stir in her raunchy outfits. Men would fall for her but she wasn't really interested – she was more into keeping fit and her quest for stardom.'

More outgoing now than ever, Geri likes to 'flash at people down the King's road for a laugh.' She is the Spice Girl most loved by older girls and gay men. Some have described her as the intellectual of the group.

Geri had loads of jobs after leaving school at 16: she has been a babysitter, a club dancer in Majorca, an office worker, an unqualified aerobics teacher, a bargirl, a hairdresser and a sales assistant at Watford's British Home Stores (where she apparently used to tell her friend Paula: 'One day I'm gonna be famous!').

She was also employed by Video Collection, where she had to check for swear words in videos. She even appeared as a games show hostess on Turkish TV's equivalent of *The Price Is Right*, posing and preening in front of the cuddly toys, stereos and beds.

Most notoriously, Geri went through a phase of 'glamour modelling' following a stint as a regular model for designer Katherine Hamnett.

Many photos have appeared over the last few months in papers and magazines. Geri first posed nude for a local photographer in her bid to become a famous model. A few years ago she was snapped topless in a failed attempt to become a *Sun* Page Three

girl. She was on the cover of 'pain and penetration' magazine *Eros*. And she apparently once said: 'I'd love to do a centrefold for *Playboy*!'

The *News Of The World* has featured naked shots of Geri posing in what looks like a parody of the 'Natrel' TV adverts. In other tabloid 'exclusives', she has been shown with her 'modesty' covered by bottles of Old Spice after-shave.

Geri's big break came when she persuaded Spice Girls' management team that she was exactly what they wanted. One of the team said: 'She didn't have the greatest voice but she kept phoning all the time saying she was what we were looking for. She had the personality – and after singing lessons we realised she really did have what it takes.'

Geri lights up London at Christmas

'One day I'm going to be famous'

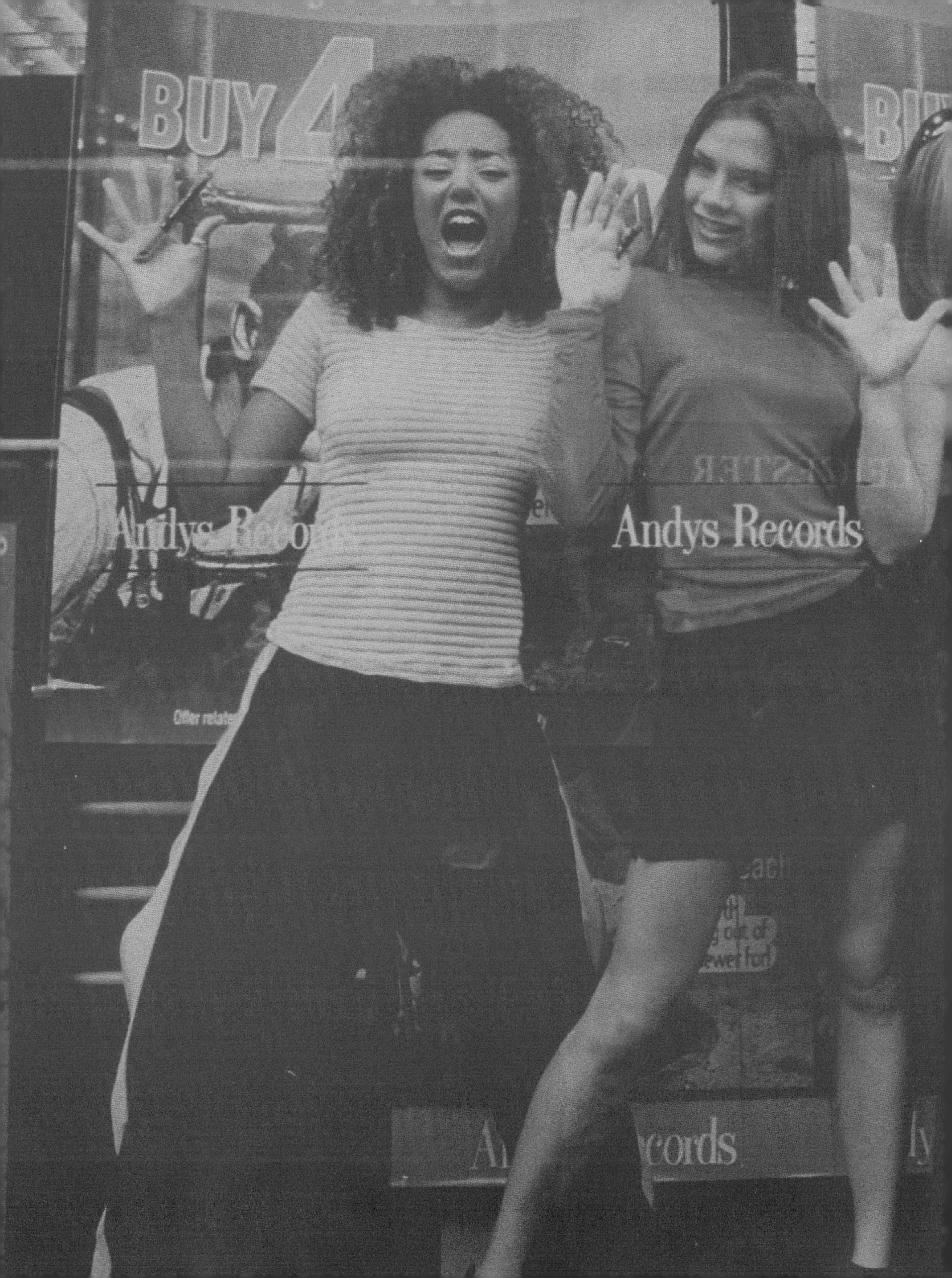
BUY 4
Andys Records

Defining the Nineties

AND SO TO WORK

It was at Kempton Park that they were spotted by Vincent Monsey of The Box, an increasingly influential cable television pop channel whose mainly teenage viewers choose which videos they want to see by voting over the phone.

'When I first saw the Spice Girls on top of a statue of Red Rum, their personalities came right through and I knew they would do something big,' said Monsey. 'They had self-propelling talent.'

And so it was that The Box, in a bid to beat the more mainstream MTV to a scoop, played the 'Wannabe' video, directed by the team behind the Diesel Jeans adverts – all cleavage, lipstick, backflips and karate kicks (remember: the girls do all their own choreography) – no less than 70 times a week in the six week run up to its release, an accolade normally reserved for top-of-the-chart records.

The irresistible rise of The Spice Girls continued apace in July 1996 when 'Wannabe' was released.

'Wannabe' was an R&B-lite/girlrap single about friendship being more important than boys. On another level, it was a post-feminist rallying cry, as representative of modern female values and attitudes as was 'Material Girl' in the Eighties.

The song was an instant radio smash, helped in no small way by the inclusion of that now irritatingly familiar new word that no one seems to know the meaning of – 'zig-a-zig-ah!'

The record, described by *Smash Hits* as 'Oasis with a Wonderbra', entered the charts at Number Three on July 20th, and then, one week later, went to Number One, making The Spice Girls the first all-girl group since The Bangles to reach pole position.

'Wannabe' stayed at Number One for seven weeks, hindering the comebacks of Gary Barlow (who got knocked off the top slot after only one week), Robbie Williams (whose anodyne version of George Michael's 'Freedom' was kept off pole position by 'Wannabe') as well as preventing George Michael's 'Spinning The Wheel' from being his third consecutive Number One of 1996.

Posh Spice meets the common people

The Girls sign on

Not that the girls have ever let hard graft get in the way of simple fun. Indeed, it was while they were writing songs with Eliot Kennedy, as well as with Matt Rowe, – one half of the writing and production team Stannard and Rowe – that the Girls got up to all sorts of media mischief at Kempton Park Racecourse.

'Hello, Mum!'

PLATINUM

'Wannabe' went on to top the charts in a further 21 countries and has since become Virgin's biggest-selling single for 13 years, topping the million mark in the UK and selling well over two million worldwide.

'Say You'll Be There', the Spice Girls' second slice of delicious swingbeat, sold 350,000 copies in the first week of its release in October, which meant that it actually debuted at Number One, helped by a video, shot in Los Angeles, which featured the girls as kung-fu kicking ultravixens.

Music paper *Melody Maker* called the record 'the most glorious pop single of the year, alongside Livin Joy's "Don't Stop Movin'" and Spice Girls' own "Wannabe".' The reviewer gave special mention to the extra track on the CD, 'Take Me Home', which was unavailable elsewhere ('Wannabe' had also included an excellent extra track called 'Bumper 2 Bumper').

Spice Girls are the first female band ever to debut at Number One, a feat which has

earned them a place in the *Guiness Book Of Records*. 'Say You'll Be There' was certified platinum in five days and is already one of the fastest-selling singles of all time. In fact, 600,000 copies were sold in one week.

If further proof were needed that Spice Girls are nothing short of a pop phenomenon, in Japan they are the biggest-selling Western act since The Beatles!

Astonishingly, in 1996, it was estimated that the group earned £10 million. Not that the girls had been able to spend any of their quickly accumulated fortune.

'People say we're worth millions,' Mel B told Louise Gannon of *The Express*, 'but we won't see any of it for ages. We get pocket money, but that's it.

'Last weekend,' she continued, 'my boyfriend and I were starving. He didn't have any money and I didn't have a penny on me. He said, "Everybody thinks you're loaded and here we are outside the shops with no money." Hopefully, this time next year, I'll be able to buy a square meal.' Aaaah.

Mel's food shortage didn't exactly dampen her, or any of the other girls', spirit in '96. In fact, they are as fierce and feisty a bunch of women as have ever crashlanded on Planet Pop.

The five girls say they stand for Girl Power, and are happy with their success after years of dominance by boy bands. They are fine examples of that marvellous species of the self-assured Nineties woman – the New Lasses.

The boys fancy them and the girls identify with them. They're smart and spontaneous, glamorous yet gritty, anarchic and abrasive. They have been described as Shampoo-meets-The Sex Pistols, and as the female equivalent of Oasis.

'They are, along with Oasis and The Prodigy, one of the bands that define the Nineties,' wrote Emma Forrest in upmarket newspaper *The Independent*. 'There is a dash of Yuppie and a dash of Page Three Girl about them. They're real Sixties dolly birds yet very Nineties.

'At other times - with Mel's untameable afro next to Emma's white blonde bunches, the half-Spanish Geri next to the Dutch Victoria – they look more like a meeting of the United Nations than a pop group.

'They're more Maybelline than Yves Saint Laurent. They're all gorgeous, but there's something rough about them.'

Geri herself put it more succinctly when she said: 'We want to bring some glamour back to pop, like Madonna had when we were growing up. Pop is about fantasy and escape, but there's so much bullshit around at the moment.'

Added Mel B: 'We want to be relevant to girls our age. Remember when Neneh Cherry first appeared on the scene? She was a ballsy, sexy woman from out of nowhere with a completely different attitude.'

METEORIC

The Spice Girls have enjoyed a meteoric rise to fame. But will it last? Will they inspire young girls to form bands and lead to a spate of Spice Girl wannabes? And what effect will they have on a new generation of young women?

'Girl Power is about respect, about showing respect,' said Geri. 'If someone shouts "Show your boobies" at a Spice Girls concert, they get thrown out immediately. We've got a serious message, we want to spread the Spice movement. We're in charge all the way.

'We're not some pre-packaged product or management-led concept,' the red-headed one continued. 'We all sing, we all dance, we all write the songs and decide on the arrangements and the way we present ourselves. We call the shots.'

She's a real lay-dee

Mel B prepares to slam her body down and wind it all around

Sunday November 24th: News Of The World

The sexy confessions of the Spice Girls, whose motto, apparently, is: 'A lover a day keeps the doctor away.'

'Sex Is The Spice Of Life For These Saucy Girls'

Monday November 18th: The Sun

'WHAT WILLS ROYALLY ROYALLY WANTS!'

A story about Prince William cruelly binning his Pamela Anderson poster and replacing it with a new bedside pin-up – of Spice Girl Emma Bunton!

Said a spokesman for the Prince: 'Wills is head-over-heels. He has consigned Pam's poster to the wastepaper basket. And he has already asked his mum if he can see them in concert.'

DAILY STAR

OOH, AAH, 15 PAGES OF SOCC-AAH!

MONDAY, DECEMBER 9, 1996   30p

WORLD EXCLUSIVE

TALK LIVE with Baby, Sporty, Posh, Ginger and Scary... TODAY!

See Page 4

SPICE GIRLS MADE MY BOY WALK

MATTHEW ACTON

A LITTLE boy who couldn't walk suddenly jumped up and started dancing — to a Spice Girls hit.

Doctors had said there was little they could do for cerebral palsy victim Daniel Williams, five.

But amazingly he stood up for the first time when he saw the Spice Girls on TV — and began to boogie with his astonished mum Paula, 32.

Miracle

"It was a miracle," she said yesterday. "Their first single, Wannabe, came on — and he was off.

"He jumped off the settee, ran over to the telly and started hugging it.

"Then he started dancing in time to the music. His little legs were going like mad.

"The next thing, he came over to me, grabbed my hand, and I started dancing with him. It was wonderful.

"To look at him you wouldn't have believed he had cerebral palsy. It was the moment we had

Turn to Page 5

Movie moguls reel 'em in   Pages 4 and 5

Monday December 9th: Daily Star

It's official! The Spice Girls can heal the sick! According to the *Daily Star*, 'a little boy who couldn't walk suddenly jumped up and started dancing – to a Spice Girls hit.'

Apparently, doctors had said there was no cure for five year old cerebral palsy victim Daniel Williams. But then, one miraculous morning, the boy, who had never walked on his own before, saw the girls performing 'Wannabe' on TV, jumped off the settee, ran over to the telly and began hugging it.

'SPICE GIRL GERI'S SECRET DUNGEON SEX PICTURES: Pop Stunna's Shocker In Black Leather And Chains'

Sunday November 24th: Sunday Sport

'MEL AS SHE USED TO B: Spice Girls star was a dancer in sleazy club'

Monday November 25th: The Sun
One of many reports exposing the 'sordid past' of Mel B

'The Ice Girls — Thaw blimey!'

Saturday November 30th: The Sun
A story about how the girls were forced to wrap up warm while shooting the video for '2 Become 1' in New York's sub-zero temperatures.

Wrote *Sun* columnist Andy Coulson: 'We are used to seeing the girls flaunting their sexy bodies in skimpy gear. But even though they had to cover up against a biting wind in the Big Apple, they still managed to stop the traffic. Cars ground to a halt for more than an hour while Mel C and Victoria were winched up for shots on the girders of the Brooklyn Bridge.'

Wednesday December 4th: The Sun
'DO YOU LOOK LIKE A SPICE GIRL?'
The *Sun* asks whether any of its readers are 'the spitting image of the Spice Girls.' If they are, then mega-fame awaits!

Tuesday November 26th: The Sun
Featuring pictures and information on 'Britain's hottest ever all-girl band when they were kids.'

MARVEL . . . Mel B

DO YOU LOOK LIKE A SPICE GIRL?

RECKON you're the spitting image of one of the sensational Spice Girls? Then let us know! Send us your photo if you look like one of the sexy all-girl group — perhaps Mel B or Geri. Include your name, age, address and a day phone number and tell us which girl you resemble. Send an SAE if you want your snap back. Write to SPICE GIRLS, The Sun, 1 Virginia St, London E1 9BD.

GORGEOUS . . . Geri

'Wannababies: The Spice Girls when they were nice girls.'

'BABY SPICE'

KNOWN AS: Baby Spice

REAL NAME: Emma Lee Bunton

NICKNAME AT SCHOOL: Emmie

NAME IF BORN A BOY: Tom

AGE: 19

BIRTHDAY: 21st January 1978

STAR SIGN: Aquarius

BIRTHPLACE: Finchley, North London

EYES: Blue

HAIR: Blonde
(worn these days in bunches or pigtails)

CLOTHES: 'Kitschy' outfits in baby blue,
baby pink, or white, made of shiny,
lacy or fluffy material

MUM AND DAD: Pauline, who runs a
self-defence club in East Finchley, Trevor,
a milkman

BROTHER: Paul James (PJ), 16

SCHOOL: St Theresa's Roman Catholic
Primary School (Emma still keeps in touch
with her former head teacher, Dennis Carey.
She was even going to open their Christmas
fête, but had to cancel due to a Spice Girls
trip to Germany)

LOVES: Hugging, love and sweets; clubbing
at The Cross or Bagley's; British beef,
bricklayers and Pina Coladas

HATES: Doughnuts with powder instead
of sugar

BAD HABIT: Picks her nose; falls asleep
too often

FAVE TV SHOW: Eastenders

MUSIC: Blur and Bobby Brown (who she
had a teenage crush on)

MOST SEXY MAN: Johnny Depp

WORST MOMENT: When she tripped over
at her first live TV performance

TATTOO/PIERCING: None ('Just me labia')

HEROINE: Her mum

HOME: Emma still lives with her mum,
although she says they're 'like flatmates'
('she's even got a picture of a Chippendale
on her wall!')

BEST PICK-UP LINE: 'Do you want some
sweets?'

Emma, the Spice Girl loved most by little girls and older men, is sweet and sassy, a chirpy schoolgirl character, a teenage Goldie Hawn, the baby of the bunch. But don't be fooled by her cute face, her fondness for doughnuts, and her pigtails: Emma's not that sweet. In fact, she can be naughty as hell. She's also a green belt in karate, so don't mess with this baby!

She was up for the part of sassy girl Bianca on *Eastenders*, and is fond of streaking, 'but only for myself – it makes you feel free, man!'

Emma once appeared in one of those Halifax TV ads where they construct a wedding cake out of people. As a child, encouraged by her mum, she modelled for women's magazines and also appeared in the Mothercare catalogue.

Said her Primary School teacher: 'She was always a happy child. She loved singing, dancing and drama and was very good at them all. She always had a smile on her face and got on well with her peers.'

Emma joined London's famous Sylvia Young drama school at 16. One former student at the academy recalls Emma as a 'power-obsessed teenager who was always full of herself and was eager to make it to the top in any way she could. Her mum pushed her all the time – it was as though she wanted her to be famous.'

Then one day at school Emma happened to see a notice advertising auditions for an all-girl band. It was the Spice Girls, and she decided the time was right to find fame. A friend says: 'She was thrilled that she got accepted. It was all she and her mum ever wanted for her. . . Somehow I knew she would make it big.'

Baby loves candy

'We know we're all mad – and we know you're with us'

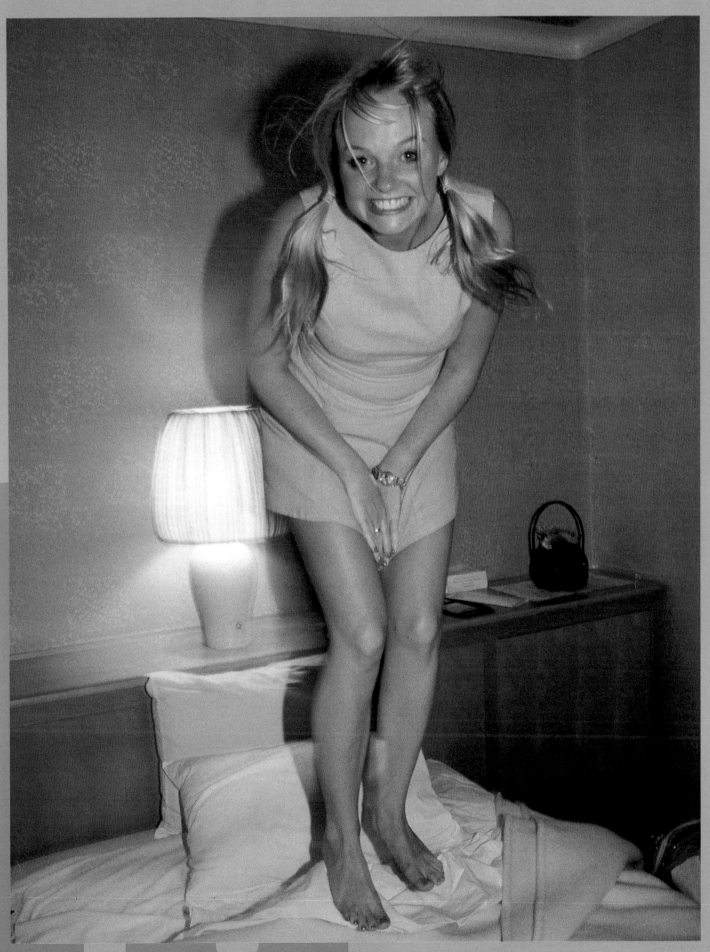

Night night, Baby!

Confessions

ON LOSING THEIR VIRGINITY:-

Emma: 'I was sixteen. It didn't all run smoothly, but it was a beautiful experience.

It was incredibly romantic. I had been dating the guy for six months and I stayed with him for a year and it got better each time.'

Geri: 'I was a really late developer at sex. But when I was 17 I did it with a guy I was totally in love with. After that I found sex so brilliant I couldn't get enough. I soon calmed down. . . a bit.'

Mel B: 'I was 15 and my parents were in the room below us. The door was locked but I was still scared they would catch me. I didn't enjoy it. It wasn't a beautiful experience. The truth is, I didn't know what to do.'

Victoria: 'I was 16 and in my boyfriend's bedroom. His mum was next door and I was terrified she would hear. It wasn't fun — it was all over so quickly, and I felt really stupid — but we soon got better.'

Mel C: 'I was 16 when I slept with a boy I was in love with. We did it while his parents were away so we could spend the whole night together. It was wonderful.'

ON SEX:-

Mel B: 'I'll try anything once. Porn or dominatrix or anything. I'm a good dominatrix. I've done private dancing, too. I feel alive when I do mad things.'

Geri: 'We don't get our knickers down straight away. If you take time out and talk to us a bit, you'll find there's a bit more behind the . . . colourfulness.'

Victoria: 'I used to get more boys interested in me before this.'

ON MALE GROUPIES:-

Mel B: 'We don't shag on the road. We never meet anybody and some of us have boyfriends. Anyway, I'd rather satisfy myself in my own room in my own way, if you know what I mean. . .'

ON FEMALE GROUPIES:-

Geri: 'Would we be interested? Probably.'

Mel B: 'I would be. I'm pretty liberated.'

ON CHAT-UP LINES:-

Mel C: 'Come on, flex your biceps, mate.'

Emma: 'Would you like one of my bonbons?'

Mel B: 'Get 'em out for the lasses!' or 'What's your naughty bit like?'

Geri: 'Make eye contact, and then. . . lunge!'

ON DRUGS:-

Mel C: 'I've never bothered.'

Emma: 'I've never been offered any. I've never tried any drugs.'

Mel B: 'We don't do drugs. We might have tried them once or twice, or we might not — we're not saying.'

Geri: 'You don't need drugs. You can get high on life.'

Mel B: 'We act like twats without drugs anyway.'

ON EACH OTHER:-

Mel B: 'We freak people out with how straight we are with each other. If someone looks shit, we'll just say, "God, you look disgusting!"'

State of the Art

Emma, Mel B and Mel C form a splinter group

The debut album by Spice Girls, simply called 'Spice', was released on November 4th, and, in its first week, unsurprisingly topped the charts and sold 160,000 copies. On a less happy note, Robson and Jerome soon knocked them off the top, as they had a few weeks before with the single 'What Becomes of the Brokenhearted?'

BITS AND BOBS

'Spice' came with a free insert which informed purchasers of the many exciting Spice Girls accessories (called 'Spice Girls Bits & Bobs') that purchasers of the 'Spice' CD could send away for, such as rucksacks, plastic keyrings, T-shirts and special 'Spicewatch' posters. The latter featured the girls dressed up, pretending to be members of the cast of Baywatch, all gleaming white smiles and red swimming costumes.

On one side of the fold-out inner sleeve of 'Spice' there were featured all manner of Spice-type slogans such as 'It's A Girls World', 'She Who Dares Wins', 'It's a Girl Thang', 'The Future Is Female', 'Silence Is Golden But Shouting Is Fun' and 'The Spice Squad Are Here'.

The other side of the CD's inner sleeve featured great new individual photos of the five girls, together with their autographs, alongside the lyrics to the 10 tracks. Next to these were the credits, which demonstrated, once and for all, that Spice Girls were no airhead floozies – they had a hand in writing the words and music to each and every one of the 10 songs on 'Spice'.

As for the music, it was far more vital and varied than anyone dared hope it would be. Apart from the 'Wannabe' and 'Say You'll Be There' singles, there was the lovely ballad '2 Become 1' (which was to be the girls'

third single), the slammin' 'Love Thing', the funkily Mary J Blige-ish 'Last Time Lover', the hip hoppy ode to mums everywhere called 'Mama', the Seventies dance-style 'Who Do You Think You Are', the fabulous Chic/Sister Sledge disco of 'Something Kinda Funny', the sultry smooch anthem 'Naked' and, last but by no means least, the scratch'n'rap grooviness of 'If U Can't Dance', which managed to outdo Neneh Cherry herself.

Come on down!

UNANIMOUS

The critics were rightly unanimous in their praise for the girls' debut album. Higbrow newspaper *The Telegraph* wrote: 'Any parent flinching at the thought of having to live with several weeks of this album on constant rotation can be assured that at least a couple of these tracks – the chattering, wah-wah-loaded Seventies funk of "Who Do You Think You Are", the slinky swingbeat of "If U Can't Dance" – will remain listenable until well after Christmas.'

The hipsters' favourite music weekly the *NME* called 'Spice' a 'state-of-the-art pop record, as good as the mainstream ever gets.' *The Times* reviewer said 'the Girls hint at a depth of feeling that goes well beyond the superficial charm of traditional teen pop. Their reward may well be success, and possibly even respect, on a scale to rival that of Oasis.'

But the most complimentary write-up appeared in new film-and-music magazine, *Neon*: 'The album successfully draws on the whole spectrum of pop history, from raunchy George Clinton sex-funk ("Love Thing") to lush Madonna-style ballads ("Mama") and even a pumping dancefloor critique of male sexual performance ("Who Do You Think You Are"). On this form, The Spice Girls are stomping all over such anaemic boy-band drones as Boyzone.'

Not bad for a bunch of girls written off by some as one-hit-wonder clothes-horses.

Pogo a-go-go!

(often spelt 'Aadams')

NICKNAME AT SCHOOL: Sticky Vicky

AGE: 22

BIRTHDAY: March 7th 1975

STARSIGN: Pisces

NAME IF BORN A BOY: Terrible Ted

BIRTHPLACE: A little village in Hertfordshire called Goff's Oak

BROTHERS/SISTERS: Louise, 19; Christian, 17

HOME: With her parents in a big converted schoolhouse

MUM AND DAD: Tony (a member of Sixties covers band The Sonics) and Jackie, who run a successful electrical wholesale business

SCHOOL: St Mary's High, in Cheshunt, Herts (where she did well in her exams)

PETS: Three Yorkshire Terriers

EYES: Brown

HAIR: Dark brown

CLOTHES: Designer

FAVE TV SHOW: She doesn't watch TV!

LOVES: Shopping, shopping and shopping; Luxury goods and designer clothes

HATES: Japanese food

met Sean Connery when she was younger, and her mum made him pretend to be James Bond!)

WORST MOMENT: Her top fell off when she was a dancer

TATTOO/PIERCING: A few earrings and a little diamond in her fingernail; she also has a pierced belly-button

WISH: To be successful!

HERO: Jack Dee

HEROINES: Anita Baker and Toni Braxton

BEST PICK-UP LINE: I just tell someone I like them

Vicki

As her name suggests, Victoria is elegant, all high heels and handbags. She is smouldering and sensual, although she has been known to snarl and smirk. In the lyrics to 'Wannabe', she is described 'a real lady'.

She is cool and classy, sultry and sophisticated, the glamour-puss of the group, with expensive tastes for such top designer labels as Gucci. A critic has called her 'Lucretia DeVille goes supermodel'; another likened her to man-hungry Dorian from the British TV show *Birds Of A Feather*!

She represents the rarely seen sulky side of the band. Men are either terrified of her or, as Geri says, 'they want to screw her.' She is always being headhunted by model agencies because of her beautiful face.

At infant and junior school, Victoria excelled at drama and dancing and loved appearing in the annual school pantomime. At 16, she pursued her dream of being famous and applied to train in theatre management at the Laine Arts Theatre College in Epsom, Surrey. She was accepted and, after completing a three-year course, she joined the cast of a small-time touring musical company.

But her real ambition was to become a singer, and when she saw an advert to join a pop group, she suddenly left the company. Vicki worked hard in this three-women, two-men band. But, just as they were poised to hit the big-time, Victoria made another sudden departure – to become a Spice Girl!

'We're not afraid to sound controversial'

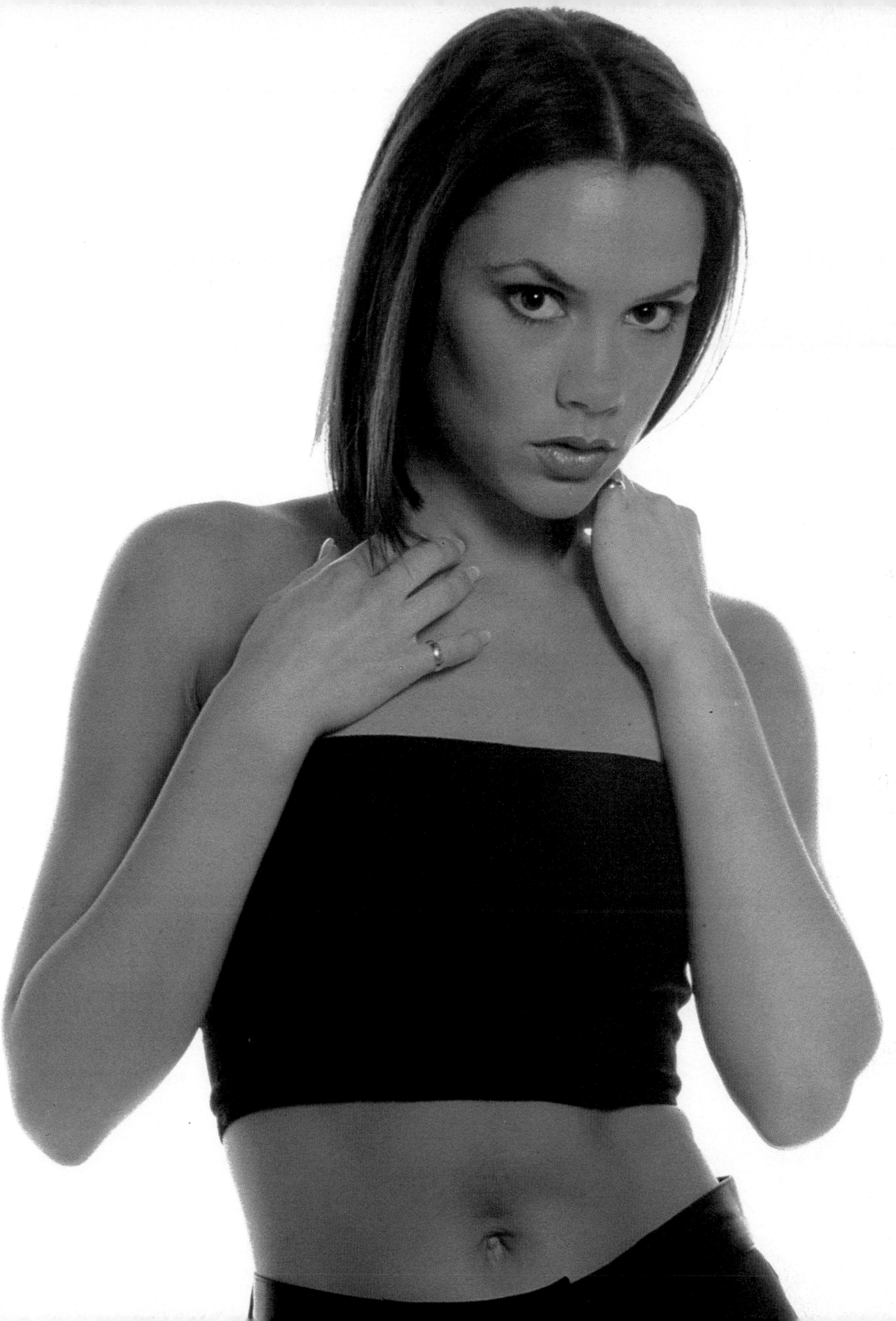

Girl Groups

Bananarama

The Beverley Sisters

The Ronettes

Three Degrees

The Spice Girls are the latest in the long line of Girl Groups, the female vocal acts who have been a part of the music scene since pop began. From the Andrews Sisters in the Forties and the UK's Beverley Sisters in the Fifties, Girl Groups really became a force to be reckoned with in the Sixties when the Ronettes, Shirelles, Supremes and dozens more – and not forgetting the legendary Shangri-Las – were never out of the charts. Through the Seventies and Eighties the likes of the Nolans, the Pointer Sisters, Three Degrees and Bananarama kept the feminine flag flying, and the Spice Girls have taken musical Girl Power a further step forward as the Millennium approaches.

The Nolans

Shangri-Las

The Pointer Sisters

Famous Friends

Courtney Love

Boyzone

Cast

Boyzone: The girls pestered them, making them embarrassed and flustered.

THE BACKSTREET BOYS: Geri once convinced the boyband popsters that she had two Ws on her buttocks, 'so it spells WOW.'

LOUISE: 'She's very quiet,' said Mel B, 'but she's got lovely breasts.'

BRAD PITT: Mel B approached him in a hotel, slapped him on the back and said, 'All right, Brad, how are you?' He just looked at her and smiled.

LENNY KRAVITZ: He shared his Jamaican takeaway with them at the Brits.

CAST: The girls met the Scally Britpoppers down at *Top Of The Pops* and tried to strangle them with a fire hose. The girls thought they were cool, though.

JAS MANN OF BABYLON ZOO: The girls met him at *Top Of The Pops* and kept saying to him, 'Oooh, Spaceman,' making him even more nervous than he already was.

AC/DC: Emma chatted up the legendary bad boys of Australian Heavy metal in a Los Angeles hotel, although she apparently didn't have a clue who they were.

BOYZONE: The girls pestered them, making them embarrassed and flustered.

PAT SHARP: Geri dashed over to the DJ with gravity-defying hair at a radio roadshow, mistaking him for DJ Mick Brown.

COURTNEY LOVE: They met the Queen of Grunge in LA, and were invited to join her in her hotel bedroom for tea.

JON BON JOVI: They met the formerly bouffant-haired rock god in Los Angeles, but were disappointed that he wasn't as good-looking in real life.

BRYAN ADAMS: Geri forced the gruff rocker to sit on her knee, and was amazed how small he was.

KULA SHAKER: The girls shouted 'show us your tits' at the posh sitar-rockers when they met them at *Top Of The Pops*.

Louise

Spice Girls with The Back Street Boys

Pollwinners

AWARDS

The Spice Girls were invited to present the award for Best Designer on BBC2's *The Clothes Show*, followed by the *Smash Hits* pollwinners party, where they won some awards of their own. At the televised ceremony, the girls performed alongside Peter Andre, Boyzone and Robbie Williams, and won awards for Best Video, Best New Group and Best British Group.

'We know we're all mad! And we know you're with us!' beamed Emma as she bounced onstage to collect the Best New Group award. 'Girl Power!' yelled Geri.

For their live rendition of 'Say You'll Be There', Geri's hair was an explosion of ginger frizz, and she was wearing a sequinned turquoise dress with a split right up the sides, as well as high heel boots. Emma had on a red short coat and boots with stack heels. Victoria wore a black leather coat, a black mini-skirt and a black shirt. Mel C stuck to her trademark Umbro sportswear. And Mel B chose a pair of bum-revealing brown hipsters and a tiny, tight bikini top.

When Lily Savage presented them with the award for Best British Group, Geri fell to her knees and did a 'we're not worthy'-style bow in front of the drag artist-cum-comedienne, saying, 'Lily's got Girl Power!'

Mel B thanked the fans for supporting them, while Geri added: 'We've got Girl Power in the house! Girl Power!' Final confirmation of their impact on the mainstream came when they were the star guests on the *National Lottery Show* on December 7th, where they performed their Christmas single, '2 Become 1'.

Giz a kiss!

'Ere, give me my gloves back!

Those boots are made for clomping!

SpiceGirls
Girls

In November the Girls turned on the Christmas lights in London's Oxford Street, outside the Bond Street HMV record store. Thousands of fans were there to cheer them on, as was Doctor Fox, the DJ from London radio station Capital FM. 'Will you be keeping your clothes on for Christmas?' Doc Fox whispered to Geri. 'Maybe I will' she purred in reply, 'but then again, maybe I won't.'

KNOWN AS: Scary Spice or Wild Spice

REAL NAME: Melanie Janine Brown

NICKNAME AT SCHOOL: Pineapple-Head (because of her frizzy hair)

AGE: 21

BIRTHDAY: 29th May 1975

STARSIGN: Gemini

BIRTHPLACE: In a small, semi-detached house in Burley, Leeds

MUM AND DAD: Andrea, a cleaner, Martin, a factory worker

SISTER: Danielle, 16

EYES: Dark brown

HAIR: Black/brown

CLOTHES: She likes jungle and soul music, so. . . Clubwear!

LOVES: Honesty. Fish & chips and junk food in general

HATES: Liars; healthy salads

MOST SEXY MAN: George Clooney ('I'm looking forward to seeing him in rubber as Batman!')

WORST MOMENT: Being discovered doing a pee in an alley

BAD HABIT: Bites her toenails

TATTOO/PIERCING: A pierced tongue ('It's meant to be good for oral sex') and a tattoo on her belly ('Something in Chinese')

WISH: An outrageous motorbike

MUSICAL HEROINES: Tina Turner and Tracy Chapman

FAVE TV SHOW: 'A programme where a girl goes to different clubs and stuff – I can't remember the name'

MUSIC: Skunk Anansie, Fugees

BEST PICK-UP LINE: 'Listen, boy: I like you; what do you think of me?'

'WILD SPICE'

Mel is proud and deafeningly loud! Along with Geri, she has the most 'bottle' of the Spice Girls. She is spontaneous (she wanted to do a 'moonie' on *Top Of The Pops*!) and generous. She is also a real party animal – she doesn't just go to one club a night, she goes to them all.

Mel is very candid ('Ask me anything,' she has said. 'I don't care'). The tabloids reported that she slept with both her neighbours and her outraged reply was: 'What a load of bollocks – one of them gave me six out of 10. Well, he obviously hadn't slept with me because he would have given me 11 out of 10!'

Ms Wild Spice once turned down G-Man from MN8, and used to go out with someone in the army – 'but it was OK because he was all chilled out by then.'

A highly experienced young woman, Mel has appeared in top TV soaps *Coronation St* and *Emmerdale*. Four years ago, when she was a hard-up, 17 year old music student, she was earning £3 an hour dancing in her bikini at a sleazy nightclub in Leeds, where she gyrated her hips and wriggled around on a podium.

Said an old friend: 'The job brought in money. She didn't have to take her bikini off, and she was performing, so she didn't mind.' Her mum Andrea added: 'She's always been the sort of girl who would only do what she wanted. She has always been headstrong.' For example, Mel went topless when she went on holiday two years ago with Geri, on a Christmas break to Gran Canaria. Holidaygoer Ralph Barber, 33, of Oldham, Lancs, said the pair were always singing and saying they were going to be famous.

Mel can play drums and used to take ballet lessons. She applied to Intake High School in Bramley, the only school in the city offering a performing arts course. Her schoolmates included Angela Griffin – who plays Fiona in *Coronation Street* – and Rebecca Callard – from Band Of Gold, the daughter of Bev Callard, who plays Liz McDonald in *Coronation Street*.

Said Bev: 'Mel and Rebecca are still firm friends. Mel was a lovely, bubbly girl and she and Rebecca just hit it off. Mel hasn't changed at all and the pair went out in London together only a few weeks ago.'

Mel left Intake at 16, then studied singing at Leeds College of Music, followed by a part-time two-year course at the Northern School of Contemporary Dance.

In 1992, when she was 17, she won a local beauty contest, with prizes of a Renault Clio for a year, a weekend for two in Paris and a modelling course. ('I'm amazed I got this far,' she said at the time.) She was cheered on by her first true love, Stephen Mullrain, now 22 – he had been a budding soccer star at Leeds United but his career was cut short at 18 by a head injury. Friends say the pair were madly in love but Mel, ever pragmatic, decided to end the relationship to pursue her career.

She kept auditioning and moved to London after she was accepted for the *Starlight Express* trainee skating school. A couple of months later, she passed another audition – for the Spice Girls.

Mum Andrea has said: 'Mel loves being in the band and it's great seeing her on telly. I'm very proud of her and how hard she's worked over the years. The downside is that I miss her a lot – but that's the price I have to pay for her success.'

'Cheese!'

'Listen, boy: I like you; what do you think of me?'

Discography

SINGLES

Wannabe b/w Bumper 2 Bumper
(Highest chart position: 1)
[VSCDT 1588]

Say You'll Be There b/w Take Me Home
(Highest chart position: 1)
[VSCDT 1601]

2 Become 1 b/w One Of These Girls & Sleigh Ride
(Highest chart position: 1)
[VSCDT 1607]

Mama b/w Who Do You Think You Are & Baby Come Round
(Highest chart position: 1)
[VSCDG 1623]

ALBUM

SPICE
(Highest chart position: 1)
[VSCDT 2812]

Track Listing:

Wannabe (Spice Girls/Stannard/Rowe)

Say You'll Be There (Spice Girls/Kennedy)

2 Become 1 (Spice Girls/Stannard/Rowe)

Love Thing (Spice Girls/Kennedy/Bayliss)

Last Time Lover (Spice Girls/Watkins/Wilson)

Mama (Spice Girls/Stannard/Rowe)

Who Do You Think You Are (Spice Girls/Watkins/Wilson)

Something Kinda Funny (Spice Girls/Watkins/Wilson)

Naked (Spice Girls/Watkins/Wilson)

If U Can't Dance (Spice Girls/Stannard/Rowe)

'SPICE GIRLS

'The Nice Girls — Spicers boost Dunblane disc.'

Saturday November 30th: The Sun
Just to show the Spice Girls are conscientious types beneath the cool exterior, here we learn how they postponed the release of '2 Become 1' to help the *Sun*-backed Dunblane record get to Number 1. The girls had planned to put out their third single on December 9th – the same day as anti-guns song 'Knockin' On Heaven's Door'. But they insisted on delaying the track by a week so the tribute record would have a better chance of hitting the top spot in its first week of release.

A spokesman for the girls said: 'We wish the Dunblane record all the success it truly deserves.'

The Dunblane record was now favourite with bookies to hit Number 1 over Christmas with odds of 8-11. The Spice Girls dropped to second favourites.
Simon Clare from bookies Ladbrokes told *The Sun*: 'The bets for the Spice Girls are beginning to dry up and there has been a real surge for Dunblane. It could be close. . .'

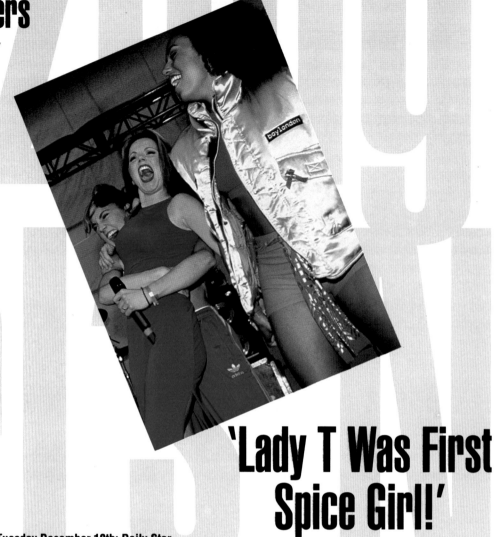

'Lady T Was First Spice Girl!'

Tuesday December 10th: Daily Star
In what is described as a World Exclusive, the Spice Girls spend a day at the *Daily Star* (the paper to write about the group first), answering readers' calls (or rather, 'chatting up fans on the *Star* hotlines'), voting for their Top 10 Hunks (George Clooney, Jamie Redknapp, Denzil Washington, David James, Matthew McConaughey, Bruce Willis, Paul Nicholls, Brad Pitt, Antonio Banderas and Val Kilmer), and meeting the 'miracle' cerebral palsy victim Daniel Williams.

Friday December 13th: The Sun
Following an interview with the Spice Girls in highbrow political magazine *The Spectator*, all the papers led with stories, taken from *The Spectator*, about the girls' political views, their opinions on Europe, the single currency, John Major ('A boring pillock - but better than the rest'), Tony Blair ('A marketing man with no ideas') and how Margaret Thatcher was their spiritual forebear ('She was the pioneer of our ideology - Girl Power').

'SPICE TO SEE YA!'

MOVIE ON UP'

Monday December 9th: Daily Star
In the same edition of the *Star*, it is reported that American movie moguls are taking a keen interest in the girls as future *femme fatales* of the silver screen. Hollywood here they come!

'Sizzling Spice Girl's Night Of Passion In Satin'

Sunday December 15th: News Of The World

'Spice Girl's Cocaine Shame'

Sunday December 15th: The People

'Geri nice two'

Thursday December 12th: Daily Star
More 'saucy' snaps of Geri wearing a latex bodysuit that leaves very little to the imagination.

Thursday November 28th: Daily Star
An article listing numerous Spice rules (always speak your mind; never let a boy muck you around; be outrageous), Spice phrases (Sod off freakface! Get mullered! Girl Power! Go play with your own balls!), Spice dos and don'ts (DO wear colour-fast lipstick if you plan to kiss a boy; DON'T be afraid to wear outlandish gear) and, finally, various ways to START A SPICE RIOT:-
- Dance on tables in restaurants!
- Cartwheel across hotel lobbies!
- Show off your pierced tongue to a waiter!
- Wear micro-skirts to posh events!
- Jiggle your assets to embarrass businessmen!

Friday December 6th: The Sport
'NUDE SPICE GIRL LOTTO SHOCKER'
Geri's nude model past is revealed on the eve of Spice Girls' appearance on family favourite *The National Lottery Show*! The shame!

Stand Up and Shout

So that's five bottles each, then!

Towards the end of the year, the Girls spent a lot of their spare time giving interviews to the press, which offered the impression that there was no more to the Spice Girls than caricature sex-kittens in Top Shop gear. 'I want people to think of us as the new Oasis', Mel C told one writer. 'Everywhere we go, people say to us "How does it feel to be the new Take That?" Take That? Fuck Off!'

SOLIDARITY

'It's just lazy journalism,' decided Geri. 'We're hardly in bed by 11 o'clock.'

'Anyway,' chipped in Victoria, 'we all write our own material, and we don't all dress the same. Plus, we're not afraid to sound controversial.'

And then, as if to emphasise the fact that they're not just manufactured pop puppets at the beck and call of sinister money-men bent on manipulating the Girls into looking and sounding like gormless bimbettes, Mel C added: 'Fucking fucked-up fuck – that's how I'd describe our year.'

They also responded to the notion that they're the female Oasis when Mel B said: 'Me and Mel C are the new Gallagher brothers!'

'Oasis are just doing what The Rolling Stones did, and the Sex Pistols,' Geri told another music paper. 'It's an accepted way of behaviour. I'm more interested in people like Marianne Faithfull and Janis Joplin.'

Geri also told fashion and style magazine *The Face*: 'I want to stand up and shout - I'm a rebel with a cause. I don't want to put men down but it's time for some strong females. Feminism has become a dirty word. Girl Power is just a Nineties way of saying it. We can strike a chord, give feminism a kick up the arse. Women can be so powerful when they show solidarity.'

They can be powerful, all right. And as depraved and debauched and downright dirty as men, too, if the feature on Spice Girls in Japan, featured in the September issue of Lads Bible, *Loaded*, was any measure.

The article followed the girls (joined by two shy, nervous 18-year-old girls from Bristol, who had won a competition on *The Big Breakfast*) to the land of the rising sun and watched, aghast yet amused, as they smoked cigars, crawled around strip bars, shouted obscenities at bemused and frightened passers-by, and generally behaved in an even more appalling manner than most beer monsters.

'Come and 'ave a go if you think you're 'ard enough!' seemed to be the girls' favourite rallying cry on the trip as journalist Jim Shelley – who had previously been dragged into the toilets of the Complex nightclub in London by the girls, to treat him to an impromptu rendition of 'Wannabe' – struggled to match the girls, beer for beer, fag for fag, outrage for outrage.

The impression given was of a bunch of girls who love each other's company, love their job, love life.

In just one night, and at one bar, the girls spent £1000. Then they went to a karaoke bar to perform versions of the James Bond song 'Goldfinger', Barry Manilow's 'Copacabana', Sister Sledge's 'We Are Family' and the theme tune from *Fame*.

The girls entertained, horrified and intimidated legions of Japanese men and women during their stay. 'People shouldn't be intimidated by us, though,' said Mel B. 'We're here for everyone. They can all be Spice Boys if they want! But we're not just here to be leered at.'

By December, the girls were Number One again, with '2 Become 1'– a single whose advance sales of 750,000 broke all previous records – and they were preparing to present the Christmas edition of *Top Of The Pops*.

Infact, they were the first group to reach Number One with their first three singles since Frankie Goes To Hollywood in 1984.

There were even articles beginning to appear in American magazines such as the ultra-trendy *Interview*, heralding the imminent release of 'Spice' Stateside.

Happiness is a zig-a-zig-ah! called Hamlet

Slurp!

PHENOMENON

At the end of 1996, the girls weren't just a pop music force to be reckoned with, however, they were a serious political force as well. On Friday December 13th, every newspaper responded to an interview in the Christmas issue of the highly respectable right wing magazine, *The Spectator*.

Titled 'Spice Girls Back Sceptics On Europe', the interview, apparently done backstage at the *Smash Hits* pollwinners party, featured the girls' views on the Labour and Conservative Parties' respective manifestos in the run-up to the General Election, their opinions on the notion of a unified Europe, on the proposed single currency for all European nations, on the Maastricht Treaty, and on various other matters that, once and for all, gave the lie to the idea that Spice Girls were dumb girls.

'Until today,' wrote the *Spectator* journalist, just after referring to 'Wannabe' as 'an anthem to Thatcherite meritocratic aspiration (the girls have called former Prime Minister Margaret Thatcher 'the first Spice Girl'), 'singing ensembles had dogmatic political programmes that took stands on traditional conservative issues like hotel suite disfigurement, groupie fornication and narcotics-dealer shopping hours. The Spice Girls have changed all that.'

How did they change all that? With radical political opinions like:

Geri: 'The whole European Federal Plan is ridiculous.'

Victoria: 'Spain is probably the best model for a monarchy.'

Mel C: 'We shouldn't be prejudiced against any background, poor or aristocratic.'

As for the leaders of Britain's two major political parties, Spice Girls were equally forthright:

'His hair's all right, but we don't agree with his tax policies,' said Geri on the subject of Tony Blair. 'He's not a safe pair of hands for the economy. He's just a good marketing man. No ideals.'

'As for Major,' opined Victoria, 'he's a boring pillock. But compared to the rest, he's far better. We'd never vote Labour.'

The response to the *Spectator* interview in the rest of the media was extraordinary, both tabloid and highbrow newspapers reprinting many of the girls' quotations and asking the question: to what extent would Spice Girls affect the next General Election, due to take place in the spring of 1997?

When the girls appeared on ITV's kids pop show *The Noise* on Saturday December 14th and were asked about their 'support' for Conservative leader John Major, Mel B was quick to play down their patronage, shouting 'Anarchy!' at the camera.

In less than six months, Spice Girls had risen to the top so fast, and with such force, that they had started to affect the way people think, feel, even vote.

It was the phenomenal end to a phenomenal year for a truly phenomenal group of girls.

Then early in January '97 it was announced that they had been nominated for no less than five prestigious BRIT awards, for Best Group, Best Newcomers, Best Single ('Wannabe') and Best Video for both 'Wannabe' and 'Say You'll Be There'.

Spice Girls' final bit of history-making was set for March '97, with the release of their fourth single, 'Mama', timed to perfection to coincide with Mothers' Day.

The single was deemed to be such a dead cert Number One that bookmakers across Britain refused to take bets on its estimated chart position ('We do want to make money, you know!' said one).

No other band in recent times had topped the chart with their first four singles.

'We always knew we were going to be an international act from the start,' said Geri, as 'Wannabe' became the highest new entry in the US charts in January.

She was right. And who would dare argue with her?